The
Circuit Writer

The
Circuit Writer

Writing with Schools
and Communities

MARGOT FORTUNATO GALT

*To my dear Elizabeth
& the creativity
I prize in yr life &
Art —
con affetto
Margot*

Teachers & Writers Collaborative

New York, New York

To the teachers and students who invited me into their
schools and shone the light of their words
on the road we all travel.

The Circuit Writer: Writing with Schools and Communities
Copyright © 2006 by Teachers & Writers Collaborative. All rights reserved. Printed in the United States of America. No part of this publication may be reproduced, stored in a retrieval system, or transmitted, in any form or by any means, electronic, mechanical, photocopying, recording, or otherwise, without prior permission of the publisher.
The permissions acknowledgements on pages vii–viii constitute an extension of the copyright page.

Library of Congress Cataloging-in-Publication Data
Galt, Margot Fortunato, 1942–
The circuit writer: writing with schools and communities / Margot Fortunato Galt.
ISBN-13: 978-0-915924-26-4 (ppk. – alk. paper)
ISBN-10: 0-915924-26-9 (ppk. – alk. paper)

2006932122

Teachers & Writers Collaborative
520 Eighth Avenue, Suite 2020
New York, NY 10018-6507

Cover photos: Margot Fortunato Galt
Cover and page design: Sylvia Ruud
Printed by Victor Graphics, Inc.
First printing

ACKNOWLEDGMENTS

Teaching is a collaborative art, but for writers-in-residence collaboration extends beyond the classroom to necessities and comforts. I owe a huge debt of appreciation to teachers, staff, students, and townspeople who went out of their way to made me feel at home as a visitor to their schools. Though I may now remember only your faces and classroom presence, I continue to be buoyed by your wisdom and friendship.

To teachers and their families and friends who became comrades in the writing of this book, I offer a special thanks. You enlarged my understanding and cheered me along. In the St. Paul Public Schools: Darlene Kunze and Al Kvaal, Norita Dittberner-Jax and Heidi Bernal, Jane Sevald and Linda Kantner, Carol Markham-Cousins and Federico Ajpop. In the Kerkhoven-Murdock-Sundburg Public Schools: Ruth Govig, Carol Thomton, and Jim Van Der Pol. At Swanville School, Kathy Detloff. At Kittson Central High School, Hallock: "Charlie" Lindberg. At Twin Bluff Middle School, Red Wing: Kari Dietrich. At Centerpoint Elementary, White Bear Lake: Sandy Harthan, John Leininger, and Karla Harding. At "High Falls" charter school: Farah Nur. Special thanks also to Crookston middle-school teacher Connie Hannesson and St. Paul Academy middle-school teacher Mary Kay Orman, who deepened my appreciation of the necessary connection between teaching the Holocaust through literature and the practice of everyday good works.

A number of writer and artist friends traveled with me in their work. Others entered the teaching thicket to help me find a way. Some did both. I thank these special friends of the writing teacher: Linda Kantner, Monica Ochtrup, Florence Dacey, Elizabeth Erickson, Deborah Keenan, Jim Moore, Margie (Margaret) Hasse, Joyce Lyon, Ken Meter, Jill Breckenridge, and Phebe Hanson. My first poetry mentor, Patricia Hampl, inspired me to think that teaching could be as enchanting as writing. The Loft Literary Center's Mentor Series in Minneapolis provided other landmark poet-teachers: Lisel Mueller and Peter Meinke.

I also owe an enormous debt to institutions that supported my residencies. First and foremost to COMPAS and its director Molly LaBerge, who pioneered one of the first poets-in-the-schools programs in the nation and for thirty years until her retirement sustained its growth with unmatchable wit and grace. To the COMPAS program directors, who guided residency programs over the years, answered my phone calls from the field, and helped make anticipated journeys delightful: Daniel Gabriel, current program director, and before that, in particular, Randolph Jennings. My lasting appreciation also goes to the Minnesota State Arts Board, whose arts-in-education program with current program director Amy Frimpong and individual artist fellowship have kept me going in more ways than one.

My residencies have sometimes involved oral history because the Minnesota Humanities Commission has provided funds for oral history projects. Jane Cunningham, at the Commission, has been a special friend to this work, specifically through a grant for a Red Wing oral history project undertaken in collaboration with the Anderson Center for Interdisciplinary Studies and the Goodhue County Historical Society. Thank you to those two institutions whose directors, poet and editor Robert Hedin at the Anderson Center and Char Henn at the Historical Society, helped immensely with information, human contacts, and fiscal management.

I hold dear the people and places who made room for me to write this book: the Ragdale Foundation, Lake Forest, Illinois; Beth Slocum and her farm near Vasa, Minnesota; the nearby Anderson Center in Red Wing, Minnesota; Joan Drury and Norcroft, her writers' retreat center for women in Lutsen, Minnesota; and the Villa Maria Retreat Center in Frontenac, Minnesota.

No one could have asked for more perspicacious editors than I was awarded in Chris Edgar and Christina Davis at Teachers & Writers Collaborative. They taught me to prune my excesses and bring out the best in these stories. Amy Swauger, Teachers & Writers director, entered during the last stages of this book and gathered it forward with aplomb. I warm with appreciation toward them all.

Working with writing and education as academic disciplines has given me perspectives I value. At Hamline University, I owe special thanks for conversations about the arts of teaching and writing to Mary Rockcastle, Deborah Keenan, Patricia Straub, and Sandy Beach in the Graduate School of Liberal Studies; and to Deirdre Kramer, Carol Mayer, Barbara Swanson,

Vivian Johnson, Barbara Elvecrog, Walter Enloe, Julie Herman, Paul Gorski, Mary Speranza-Reeder, Marcia Rockwood, and Terri Christenson in the Graduate School of Education. Thanks also to Mary Diaz, jointly at Hamline Graduate School of Education and the Wisconsin Center for Education Research at the University of Wisconsin-Madison.

Finally to my family who put up with my residency absences for many years. Special thanks to my teacher daughter Alexis, who read the manuscript of this book and offered a fine critique, and to my husband Fran, veteran of many trips and revisions, lover of word games and books, and frequent caretaker of our many cats. I am grateful for your glad welcomes.

The Circuit Writer: Writing with Schools and Communities was funded by a grant from the National Endowment for the Arts.

Teachers & Writers Collaborative programs are made possible in part by grants from the New York State Council on the Arts, the New York City Department of Cultural Affairs, the Manhattan Borough President's Office, and the Manhattan City Council Delegation.

Teachers & Writers Collaborative is also grateful for support from Bydale Foundation, Carnegie Corporation of New York, Cerimon Fund, Consolidated Edison, E.H.A. Foundation, Agnes Gund & Daniel Shapiro, Heckscher Foundation, Jeannette and H. Peter Kriendler Charitable Trust, JP Morgan Chase Foundation, New York Times Company Foundation, David Rockefeller Fund, The Scheide Fund, Smith Barney (Citigroup Foundation), Starbucks Foundation, Steele Reese Foundation, Verizon Foundation, and members and friends of Teachers & Writers Collaborative.

Teachers & Writers Collaborative is grateful for permission to reprint the following material. James Moore for "That Summer, for Marijo." Kate Green for "Don't Make Your Life Too Beautiful." Spoon River Poetry Press for "Old Man Brunner Spearing Carp on Wolf Creek" and "How to Take a

CONTENTS

While Fancy, like the finger of a clock,
Runs the great circuit, and is still at home.
—William Cowper[1]

In the mid-1960s, while I was working at Doubleday Anchor Books and pursuing a master's degree at Columbia University, a group of educators and writers began agitating to reform public education in a way that would ultimately change the course of my life. Not exactly Sputnik-inspired, but starry-eyed with reforming zeal, New York writers like Kenneth Koch, Grace Paley, and June Jordan founded Teachers & Writers Collaborative in 1967, based on the belief that poetry writing could reclaim kids' creativity and keep them in school.[2] Meanwhile, in Minneapolis, a city that would later become my home, Molly LaBerge, with a grant from the National Endowment for the Arts through the Academy of American Poets, found matching funds "out of the night" and inaugurated a poetic partnership with the Minneapolis Public Schools. Nine well-known poets—Denise Levertov, Galway Kinnell, Donald Hall, and May Swenson among them—each gave standing-room-only public readings at the University of Minnesota's Bell Museum. Then local poets visited area high schools, reading in auditoriums packed with students.[3] The results were electric. Shortly thereafter, Leonard Randolph of the National Endowment for the Arts followed up on these poetry pilot readings by funding full-fledged poets-in-the-schools programs across the country. These programs, including COMPAS[4] in Minneapolis, introduced creative writing to the next generation in ways that had never before been considered in American education; poets-in-the-schools programs (later expanded to writers in the schools) were also instrumental in supporting America's emerging authors. Garrison Keillor, then a nobody with designs on publishing in *The New Yorker*, received a residency from COMPAS. He said later that it was the first real writer's income of his life.

After living in Charleston, South Carolina, Baltimore, and New York City, I moved to Minnesota in 1968, just as the war in Vietnam was linking the Hmong people of northern Laos to what would become their 1980s immigration to Minnesota. Chicano families, former migrants working Minnesota farmland, were settling in the Red River Valley. Communities on the move, from northern Ojibwe to southern African Americans, mixed and diversified the state's population. It was an exciting time, a prologue to ever-widening shifts in older German and Scandinavian populations and the clans of Poles, Finns, Italians, and Greeks on the Iron Range. By the twenty-first century, Minnesota's social service policies and programs and its religious and philanthropic outreach would draw people from all corners of the globe, including refugees from the Horn of Africa.

More immediately apparent to me was a shift in temperatures, literal and literary. As I acquired an Army-surplus parka and fur-lined boots, the Minnesota literary arts were vying with hockey for a place on the regional logo. It's hard to say what emboldened the pen: Vietnam War protests, feminism, and introspective Scandinavian culture all provided motive and direction. Suffice it to say that by the time I looked outside academe for work in the late 1970s, prairie-style literature had taken to the road in a poetry bus. In lofts, on college campuses, or at anyone's kitchen table, poets and writers drew up chairs and declared themselves organized. My first poems were published in a University of Minnesota student magazine and a mimeographed poetry rag. Poetry was declaimed on street corners and in protest demonstrations. At The Loft Literary Center in Minneapolis, I volunteered, taught, and later administered programs, and the Lake Street Writers Group, associated with the small press *Lake Street Review*, put a prairie-style simplicity to my more ornate aesthetic. From the west, on his farm near the South Dakota border, Robert Bly's literary magazines named after the decades starting with *The Fifties*, drew national attention to Midwestern writers (James Wright, Bly himself).[5] Bly's magazine also increased our knowledge of European and South American surrealists. After reading Pablo Neruda, lots of Minnesota writers began declaring that they hoped and prayed to see purple, green, and orange cows in their imaginary barns.

With all this literary ferment, it's not surprising that by the time I began making the "circuit" as a Minnesota poet-in-residence, the general writers-in-the-schools philosophy had expanded from its basic democratic premise—to take poetry out of the ivory tower and read it to kids—into an outright populist credo: the belief that the germ of poetry lay in the teachers and students themselves. The poetry we taught in the Minnesota and Dakota programs had been shaped by the confessional poetry of Robert Lowell, Sylvia Plath, and Anne Sexton,[6] which poured an elixir of permission, especially for middle-school poetic confessions. Memory poems were encouraged by Minnesota poets—my favorites Patricia Hampl, Jim Moore, Phebe Hanson, and Deborah Keenan[7]—along with visiting New York poets Ron Padgett, John Ashbery, and others. As I listened to or read their work, my childhood memories revived and I matched poems about Halloween kimonos, doll carriages, and teacups with students' prairie-attic poems, reminiscent of childhood visits to my North Dakota grandfather. William Blake's "The Tiger," along with lots of other classic poems, could inspire kids, insisted Kenneth Koch, and we proved him right.[8] Poets like Neruda and Federico Garcia Lorca, or the eighth-century Chinese poet Tu Fu, sped landlocked Minnesota students across oceans, into interior landscapes previously inaccessible to flatlanders. There was also plenty of local inspiration, like James Wright's Minnesota poem "The Blessing," which began watching horses outside Rochester, Minnesota, and ended, "... if I stepped out of my body I would break/into blossom."[9] Such lyricism, expanding into gentle, cosmic transcendence, evoked the prairie, where sky meets land wherever the eye can see.

The more I traveled from school to school, the more I understood that schools reflect the cities or small towns or rural areas they serve; schools themselves are mini-communities. They not only shape their students, they are vital to an entire town's or neighborhood's sense of unity and purpose. In small towns, for instance, almost everything happens at school, from voting to little theater, from band concerts to school athletics, from flea markets to carwashes. When population declines and a school must close, the town may feel acutely the loss of its core. Even moving a high school from Main Street to the edge of town may disrupt how a community relates to the school and, thus, to a sense of its history and identity. Big, shiny, and impersonal, the new building is too far away to reach on foot. Sudden changes in student composition—such as the arrival in the late 1990s of hundreds of East African immigrants in the Twin Cities—can also dramatically alter school communities. Though schools may have second-language programs, they may not be prepared for the effects of the hardships such refugee students have endured. Some school communities cope, as do the new immigrants, because both groups have good leadership and outside support; other immigrants and schools don't do so well, especially if their surrounding community lacks understanding.

Creative writing can foster open-minded, tolerant vitality. I've seen it work with all of the situations mentioned above. It's not like a shot in the arm; the recovery takes longer than overnight. Rather, it's like the regular return of the traveling judge or preacher who served an earlier circuit, an outsider who has visited many other schools and perceives when standardized curriculum fails to address particular needs. This sympathetic guide, removed from local associations, can often help children spring open hidden truths. Writing ushers in the strange and unexpected, yet it also speaks the universals we share. It creates its own arena, where we pause to listen and remember. One person speaks, but sparks light up in everyone's private darkness. Soon the place is ablaze with connections.[10] I remember seeing a stuttering boy who insisted he wanted to take part in his school's public poetry reading. The teacher and I held our breaths. Not only did he read without a hitch, but his lyric accomplishment outshone all others. Here was new talent and courage; his school community would not look at him the same way again.

The following chapters will focus on particular cases from my Minnesota and Dakota teaching. The geographic, economic, and historical content of these places is decidedly local, but writing is universal and teachers are scavengers. They make use of scraps; they rewire with metaphors. They welcome the chance to watch their students under a new hand, the chance to pause and explore their own stories. I'll keep my experiences succinct and as vivid as possible. I will describe real schools or community settings, a classroom or library, a park or a parking lot. Classroom exercises will be clear and straightforward. Some cases will be urban, some rural; some elementary, some older; some traditional public school, some new charter school.

And the circuit writer? She keeps returning to the circuit, leaving home on a Sunday afternoon to drive halfway across the fourteenth-largest state in the nation. Following directions to Red Wing, New Prague, Hallock, Grand Marais, she checks into a motel for an early rise to follow vague directions across snowy fields. Though a stranger in town, she carries a house on her back. It has two doors, labeled "school" and "poetry." Its windows look out to new faces and into her own past. Only with kids does she dare sing out loud. Their creative writing brings up richness no one knew they had. No poem can be wrong. With them, she will never grow old.

NOTES

[1]William Cowper, *The Task: A Poem in Six Books* (1785).

[2]Philip Lopate, editor, *Journal of a Living Experiment: A Documentary History of the First Ten Years of Teachers & Writers Collaborative* (Teachers & Writers Collaborative, 1979). A must read for anyone interested in the early days of one of the first writers-in-the-schools programs.

[3]Norita Dittberner-Jax, *Particular Gifts: A History of the COMPAS Writers-in-the-Schools Program, 1968–1988* (COMPAS, 1987). This brief history, written by a second-generation writer-in-the-schools, described Minnesota's ground-breaking Art of Poetry, a precursor to Poets in the Schools and to COMPAS. Norita, friend and colleague, is now high school language arts coordinator and a literacy coach for the St. Paul Public Schools. Her poetry is published in *What They Always Were* (New Rivers Press, 1995).

[4]COMPAS, Community Programs in the Arts, was founded in 1974 and directed for many years by Molly LaBerge. It is now located in the Landmark Center in St. Paul. I interviewed Molly in August 2004. Now retired from COMPAS, she pioneered models for presenting poetry to teachers and students that became the basis for many later poetry and writers-in-the-schools programs. COMPAS soon expanded from its original focus on writing residencies to many other programs linking arts and communities.

[5]Robert Bly, *The Light around the Body* (Harper & Row, 1967). This National Book Award winner, along with Bly's other early volume of poetry, *Silence in the Snowy Fields* (Wesleyan University Press, 1962), helped me hear Midwestern cadences and tuned me to Bly's exquisite metaphors and anti-war ironies.

[6]Robert Lowell, *Life Studies* (Vintage Books, 1959). I didn't come to Lowell until the 1970s, when this volume of confessional poetry affected me like an electric shock.

Sylvia Plath, *Ariel* (Harper & Row, 1965). Plath's poetry of motherhood and madness awed and fascinated me. I never used her work with K–12 students but did teach it in adult continuing education poetry courses. Her novel *The Bell Jar* struck common chords with my own work in New York publishing, but its account of a young woman's descent into madness demonstrated that I was boringly sane.

Anne Sexton, *To Bedlam and Part Way Back* (Houghton Mifflin Company, 1960). Like Plath's poetry, Sexton's, with its raw outrage and clairvoyant linking of female madness with gender politics, drew me like a moth to flame. Even now, years later, I feel the fascination of having my wings singed.

[7]Patricia Hampl, *Woman before an Aquarium* (University of Pittsburgh Press, 1978). James Moore, *The New Body* (University of Pittsburgh Press, 1975). Phebe Hanson, *Sacred Hearts* (Milkweed Editions, 1985). Deborah Keenan, *Household Wounds* (New Rivers Press, 1981).

The impulse toward personal memories in poetry was large; I could name dozens of Minnesotans whose memory poems I read and appreciated. Many were published in *25 Minnesota Poets*, Seymour Yesner, editorial director, Minneapolis Public Schools (Nodin Press, 1974). This anthology, along with *25 Minnesota Poets #2* (Nodin Press, 1977), introduced me to the poetry of many who worked in Minnesota poets-in-the-schools programs. These anthologies accompanied me on residencies for years, and I grew to admire the poems and eventually to become friends with some of the poets: the four whose individual works are mentioned above and, in addition, Jill Breckenridge, Margaret Hasse, Alvaro Cardona-Hine, and Joe Paddock.

Another book that I carried into K–12 classrooms throughout the 1980s was *A Geography of Poets: An Anthology of the New Poetry*, Edward Field, editor (Bantam Books, 1978). An anthology arranged by the poets' regional affiliations, this taught me about Midwestern poets who were not Minnesotan.

[8]Kenneth Koch, *Wishes, Lies, and Dreams: Teaching Children to Write Poetry* (HarperCollins, 1970). Koch's reports of teaching in New York City's PS 61 made this book hard to resist. Along with his later volume *Rose, Where Did You Get That Red?* (Vintage, 1973), Koch's work provided a necessary guide for writers new to poetry in the schools.

[9]James Wright, *Collected Poems* (Wesleyan University Press, 1951, 1971). Wright's career intrigued me with its shift from formal, jewel-like poetry to the more open, lyrical, and sometimes confessional work of his Minnesota period. Since I came from a non-Midwestern aesthetic myself, I found his shift instructive. And I unfailingly responded to poems like "The Blessing."

[10]Mark Vinz, editor, *An Explosion of White Petals: An Anthology of Student Poetry from the Minnesota Poets-in-the-Schools Program, 1978–1979* (COMPAS, 1979). One of the earliest of COMPAS's yearly student anthologies, the student writing in this anthology inspired my teaching for years. Editor Mark Vinz, an early poet-in-residence, also edited a literary magazine called *Dacotah Territory*. When I was teaching my first COMPAS residency outside Moorhead, Minnesota, Mark provided a sympathetic local guide. As the COMPAS anthologies continued publication, I would edit the 1980–81 volume, *When It Grows Up You Say Goodbye to It*, and *Give Me Your Hand* in 2000. By then, the COMPAS residency program had long since expanded from its single focus on poetry to other literary genres and art forms. It is now known as Writers & Artists in the Schools (WAITS).

CHAPTER ONE

The Road to Swanville:
Rural Towns and Consolidated Schools

I.

It was the last Monday in January 1995, 7:30 A.M. I had just left Little Falls, the hometown of aviator Charles Lindbergh, heading west on glare ice so thick across the road that it gleamed in a frozen sheet. As I approached Swanville, whose K–12 school had hired me for a weeklong writing residency, bits of other rural-town residencies over the years cut loose from their moorings to swirl around me.

Rush City: No heat in my room on the top floor of an old hotel; odors of pork and sauerkraut wafting up from the knotty pine dining room.

Granite Falls: I never made it to the Upper Sioux Agency on the Minnesota River, one of two Indian agencies attacked in August 1862 by Dakota warriors who resented the loss of land and the late shipment of food due them under U.S. government treaties. This six-week mini-war in the midst of the Civil War is rarely taught outside Minnesota, though it cruelly defined the future for many Dakota; thirty-eight were hanged in Mankato, and hundreds of others were deported to a reservation in Nebraska.

Warroad on Lake of the Woods: I visited tiny Angle Inlet school, boasting a mere seven to ten students.

Long Prairie: Where poet and English teacher David Bengtson hosted the program and his extracurricular Red Plaid Thermos Writers Clud. (The student writers' club, mistyped by David in its inaugural naming, was henceforth dubbed "Clud.") At their tongue-in-cheek bimonthly meetings Clud members would raise a thermos of Tang to toast literature and the mysterious all-powerful Bob Bergstrom (David's alias), who as president never managed to attend a meeting.

Country people sometimes give offhand directions. "Oh, you'll see it!

Come in the back way." First thing Monday morning, those directions landed me somewhere shy of Swanville, fog and snow throwing a scarf around a conglomeration of low buildings. No indication of a school, no hint of a driveway. I gripped the wheel and slowed to a crawl, until suddenly a swaying orange behemoth of a school bus came along the road and led me to the parking lot and the back door, where contact teacher Kathy Detloff was waiting. (The "contact teacher" is the scheduler and arranger of comforts for a resident artist.)

During our tour of the building, I hazarded a question about Swanville's name: "Are swans frequent visitors to Swanville?" It so happens that I once wrote an article about Minnesota's reintroduction of trumpeter swans. If the ground around Swanville hadn't been snowed in, I might have recognized the trumpeters' preferred "potholes" (Minnesota parlance for *tiny glacial lakes*). Though Kathy knew of no swan sightings, she was delighted that I wanted to try a swan-related exercise with my first class of fourth-grade students. To begin, I encouraged them to stand and stretch out their arms. "Add a foot or two at each end," I instructed. Waving my paltry 5' 4" pinions, I added that humans' wingspans tended to be equal to their height. "There aren't many people who have wingspans as long as trumpeters' seven feet." The kids giggled and flapped obligingly. As they began to loosen up, I told them, "Trumpeters once resided in Minnesota in huge flocks, but they were shot because ladies in Europe liked their long white feathers and gloves made of their skin. The swans made easy targets. You would too, if you had to flap seven-foot wings to take off."

Kathy proved to be a bundle of energy, one of those dedicated rural teachers who exemplify a truth about small-town life: everybody does everything. I first encountered this phenomenon during circuit writing days in the 1980s. In Catherine Barner's wonderfully sunny, geranium-filled classroom at Battle Lake, senior boys wrote poetry without complaint and senior girls bragged about fixing their own cars. Farmers acted in town dramas, and shopkeepers doubled as county farm extension agents. Small towns don't have enough people to specialize, Catherine explained. If a community wants a theater and several choirs and a weekly newspaper and book clubs, then everybody has to take part. Early immigrant farmer families made their own equipment, built their own houses and furniture,

sewed aprons or dresses from floral-decorated flour sacks. Living the typical seven miles from a town (the distance a team of horses could pull a
wagon to town and back for a day's shopping), rural families created their
own institutions, entertained themselves with school sings, storytelling,
game playing, and fiddling. Rural electrification did not reach many
Minnesota farm families until the 1950s, and some one-room school-
houses endured through the mid-twentieth century. Though electricity
and consolidated schools have prevailed, self-sufficiency remains an un-
spoken ethic.

After the swan warm-up, I introduced one of my favorite break-the-ice
exercises, the Surreal Photo Poem. Over my many years of circuit writing,
I've found that this exercise offers me a neutral, anonymous medium by
which to gauge the preoccupations of the students and their fields of refer-
ence. In turn, the photographs provide the students with a somewhat dis-
orienting but concretely accessible visual image to work with: a hoe just
about to settle into the earth, a train just about to depart. With ease, the
students might slide into the next narrative instant, wipe a bead of sweat
from their brows. Acquired from thrift shops and estate sales, the photographs' Midwestern references are unmistakable: a trio of youths waving
goodbye to Duluth from a caboose; stately studio portraits with garlands,
plinths, and painted backdrops; soldiers sporting ranger-style hats and cav-
alry boots outside a typical small-town train station with a roof like a ship's
hull. Other photos hail from far-off regions: Pueblo villagers in New Mexico; African American farmers jitterbugging in Clarksdale, Mississippi,
circa 1947. These, along with images of American Indians from the nine-
teenth century, had instant appeal, the fascination of the different tugging
at imagination.

The students hurried to select a photograph, usually on impulse, but
once at their desks, they entered into an intimate, if short-lived, dialogue
with the image. The quirky restrictions of old-time cameras added to the
photos' curiosity. I reminded the students that slow shutter speeds meant
that subjects had to sit still for several minutes, a far cry from a Kodak moment. Formal portraits were taken in studios with fancy props. Women often stood because they wanted to show off their elaborate hand-made
dresses. Traveling photographers would come to town or field (much like a

circuit writer) and take snapshots outdoors, with the tripod unsteady on the rough ground. As students looked at their chosen photographs, I asked them to consider what occasions had inspired them. Had the man in doughboy uniform returned from the trenches of France? Was this his daughter's only picture of him? Were the three women sisters? Was one of them getting married? Who was the seamstress of their dresses? When the photo only hinted, it was up to the writer to fill in the gaps.

To make the shift from sight to insight, from observing to writing, I encouraged the class to drape one of their own memories (or a historical fact) around a figure or object in the photo. For example, I told them that when I had measles, my father brought me a stuffed lamb from his job at the Red Cross. So, I might integrate that detail into the otherwise unknown life of a mother depicted in one of the photographs: "The woman carrying the baby in the crook of her arm remembers having measles when she was four, remembers the black lamb her father brought her." The possibilities of this kind of conflation were legion, potentially strange. The photos acted like dreams, and we became the dreamers. The student poems that emerged from this conjunction were quite different from poems about lived personal experience or remote imaginings.

Fifth/sixth-grader Jeremy H. wrote ostensibly about a curly-haired dog. Ignoring the studio backdrop of castle and clouded sky, and the plaid blanket under the dog, however, he chose to dwell on elements that led into an outer world not so different from the woods and fields surrounding Swanville. He also embedded questions within the poem itself, as I had recommended. Sometimes a question is the greatest lesson a poem can teach, and often more believable than a single-minded answer.

> The dog of the house sits on a table
> while the master dreams a dream
> of a flying bed which will take him anywhere.
> Anyhow through the door lies the dog
> looking and looking for his bone.
> The wilderness is waiting for the
> dog and the man. Who is next? Now, no
> one, no how. Who is in the woods?
> A crow, a deer, or maybe nothing,
> just the smell of a flower or two,

just to enjoy the midnight
bloom. What a day, a day for you and all.

Who else wants to be in the
place? The dog gets up and wakes his
master. Who is going and
what do you want? A walk in the woods,
I see. Some fun this will be.

Wilderness call.

Tenth-grader Katie K. chose to write about a woman whose scrawny
neck did not fit her homemade dress. At first, I thought that Katie had over-
looked the cumbersome clothing, which I had taken to be the main interest
of the image. But as I examined the photo more closely, I found a wreath
and a candle accompanied by a printed greeting, "Holiday Wishes," yet the
photo clearly celebrated her bouquet of daisies and a return of spring in an
older woman's life. It was this subtle incongruity that Katie captured: the
memory of a child standing beside her stove could have been Katie with her
own grandmother.

This little old lady
stands by the steps
wearing her best of dresses
holding the most beautiful flowers.
She fixes her shiny gray hair
to fit her egg-shaped head.

I see her standing by the stove
waiting for the sweet soft cooking to get done.
There is a small boy standing by her
smiling like the cool breeze on your face.

She stands on a ground filled with ivy flowers.
This big old white shack to take up
the background.
The boy who was once little
is now grown full.
Stands with the camera
ready to take a picture of
the most beautiful woman.

The Surreal Photo Poem Exercise

Step 1. Choose an anonymous old photo; discuss restrictions of old cameras. Discuss how clothing styles, vehicles, and other elements help define an era. Hint: Civil War and after, hoop skirts; 1880s–1910s, Gibson Girl hats with wide curving brims and dashing feathers, leg-o'-mutton sleeves, long skirts and high-button shoes, men's caps with short bills; 1910s–20s, knickers for boys and long black stockings for girls; 1920s–30s, men's felt fedoras or straw "boaters" for young dandies.

Step 2. Have students imagine the occasion for their photos. Some are easy: men holding up rabbits and guns. For difficult ones, students should guess about relationships, setting, time.

Step 3. Make a list of elements in the photo. Begin with "Where does your eye go first?" List even insignificant details of clothing, posture, gestures, expressions, hairstyles, backdrops or backgrounds; objects like a shotgun, basket of greens, or horse and buggy standing by the gate.

Step 4. Give a personal memory to someone in the photo. Or adapt a detail from history. Write what this person regrets, dreams, senses (mention the five senses), enjoys, is afraid of.

Step 5. Decide what happened just before the photo was taken and what will happen as soon as the shutter clicks. Keep the historic era in mind; imagine only what would fit that era. Perhaps the family had driven out to see their "homestead claim," dressed in their Sunday best.

Step 6. To increase surprising combinations, write a list of possible additions to the poem: an odd color, a line from a song, favorite food for people 100 years ago—i.e., not pizza. Add a natural detail: meteor shower, grasshopper chirping by the road. Add a tiny action: pouring cream from a flowered cream pitcher. Tailor poems to a particular community by including events familiar to everyone in town: a tornado, a milk truck tipping, Halloween pranks. Local audiences, who hear these poems read aloud, will appreciate these elements.

Step 7. Select the point of view that will dominate the poem: someone in the photo, or the photographer, or an onlooker who doesn't appear in the photo. A tree, a dog, a buggy—all could provide a point of view.

Step 8. Start to write by describing a small detail. Alternate description with action, memories, thoughts, and emotions. Ask questions that raise elements of emotion in oblique ways. Keep returning to details from the photo. Make a few unusual combinations; mix the familiar with the unexpected.

As a circuit writer, I like to draw upon my role as The Stranger to elicit what is familiar to the students, to help them perceive, appreciate, and articulate the time and place in which they live, from a slight remove. For my Swanville students, the photo poem exercise was just the beginning. The next day, two Swanville old-timers, Wilma Hahn and Parker Johnson, dropped by to volunteer themselves as participants in my Oral History Dramatic Monologue exercise. The exercise started out with more of a whimper than a bang, due to the fact that the students failed to muster many questions. But they weren't to blame. You don't have to see the movie *Fargo* to know that northlanders are a wonderfully reticent lot. The common Minnesota hug is A-frame, and visitors from other regions often complain that Minnesotans have a porch to their attitudes—that is, they're slow to argue or interfere. They call this "Minnesota nice," but when it comes to tenth-graders early on a winter morning, it can feel, to an anxious outsider, like "Minnesota ice." The older presence of Irish and African Americans and more recent arrival of Hispanics and Somalis have contributed to a general thaw, but there is still a pervasive sense of restraint.

That's why, whenever I'm teaching in a town that contains many generations still living in the same area, I try to encourage oral history interviews. Fielding questions not only is therapeutic for the older generation, but the stories that emerge fill crucial gaps in children's knowledge. These conversations contribute to a larger, more inclusive sense of humanity. Let's face it, even on farms or in houses in rural towns, family conversations have been nosed aside by scheduled activities, television shows, and telephone conversations. I like to sit us down together for forty minutes and listen to how older people have shaped their lives.

Instead of requiring the students to take detailed, journalistic notes during interviews, I suggested that they simply jot down the phrases that gave them pleasure. This aphoristic note-taking helped them pay attention by giving them an individual motive for listening. It also helped them let go of their preoccupation with narratives that flow from event to event, and encouraged them to listen to the patchwork way stories are actually told, shifting from physical descriptions to snippets of conversation to off-the-cuff jokes to in-depth vignettes. If we told the story of our own lives once a day for three days, I said to them, different details and emphases would emerge.

Wilma was born in the 1920s and moved from Illinois to a township fifteen miles from Swanville before first grade. Her one-room school held eight grades. "Since the teacher boarded a mile away," she explained, "she asked me to start the fire first thing in the morning." The round, wood-burning stove took an hour to heat up, so students wore their coats and hats for early-morning lessons. Wilma's mornings began well before school, as she rose at dawn to set traps for weasels in the woods. She'd bait a long line with chicken livers and string it across bushes. With her dad's help, she'd stretch and dry the pelts, then bundle them off to Sears Roebuck. "According to their size, I earned fifty cents to one dollar," she said. Wilma's evening duties included the preparation of chamber pots and Saturday-evening baths made of melted snow. "We changed the water," she added, "but not for *every* person." From November to March, her whole family wore long johns. Girls had it particularly rough, with long black stockings held up by garter belts. "The first day they fit to your leg"—Wilma crinkled up her nose—"then they started to sag. We wrapped them around our legs, which made a lump behind." She laughed at the unsightliness.

Her contemporary Parker Johnson remembered one-room schools at Bearhead, Pillsbury, Cyrus, and Vida, all of which were eventually gathered into Swanville School. Mrs. Chambers, his first teacher, "didn't like me from the day I walked in," he said, "though I didn't do nothing wrong." Often just in time for recess, she'd identify some infraction he'd committed. "Parker, you can stay in," she'd say. He shook his head ruefully. "Discipline in those days was *anything* the teacher wanted. She could whang you over the head with a book, or hit your hand with a ruler." Parker made as if he were still smarting, then smiled, recalling his subsequent spitball exploits when the teacher's back was turned. "There were as many devils those days as there are now," Parker remarked, "but I knew the teacher knew it was me." The fourth-graders laughed aloud. "The teacher said, 'Give me that peashooter,'" Parker continued. "I denied I had it, laughed, then hung onto my seat. She pulled the three of us [boys sitting together] up by our hair and our seats came along too. Then she dropped us." The fourth-graders gasped. They weren't used to adults doling out such punishments. "It took me eleven years to go eight grades," Parker confessed. "And I didn't dare complain to my dad about the discipline because I was scared of getting another round from *him*."

The next day my goal was to connect Wilma's and Parker's more distant accounts of their youth to the students' own experience of childhood—a crucial connection that was best made subtly. I didn't want to shift attention away from the speakers, yet the students needed to get inside Wilma's and Parker's experiences and claim an affinity if they were ever going to be able to write a poem. Poems, with their compression and lightning leaps, counteracted the oral interview's tendency to wander and hem and haw. That's one reason I chose poetry rather than short stories for the students' responses. In fact, using oral history material, students often blurred genres, writing short-short poem-stories. These hybrids gave us a chance to discuss differences in genres and ways students could develop their first drafts into either shorter poems or longer stories. Or, if they chose, leave them the way they were.

To initiate poems from the interviews, I reached for Midwestern poet Jim Moore's "That Summer, for Marijo," the opening word of which ("sometimes") offered a compelling gateway (a casual equivalent to "once upon a time") to student poems:

> Sometimes we played tennis,
> sometimes we sat in the dust and planned our birthdays.
> I was in love with the blonde one.
> How many evenings
> we sat on the porch
> and dusk handed over the dark
> to all of us kicking our legs under the swing.
> The horses we pretended to ride were really bicycles.
> But the love was truly love.
> Whoever we are now
> we once walked the white line of the tennis court
> one after the other with our arms held out for balance.

The brick streets were ours!
O, the thick shadows of those elms.
No other childhood is possible.
It is too late to change the name
on the gravestone of a single leaf.[1]

The students found the poem very liberating. Jim's erratic catalogue of memories gave them free rein to leap from one detail to another and showed them the cumulative impact of a seemingly random list. Because lists can grow unwieldy, I encouraged them to end their poems, much like Jim's, with an image that indicated the passage of time. Fourth-grader Rick S's poem about Wilma's life sped up her laconic presentation with short line breaks, and drew us into the experience by shifts into present tense. The highlight of badger shooting played immediately into repetitive action, which prepared for the distancing of the ending.

Wilma's Life

Sometimes I
had to feed
the cows, chickens
and sheep after
school. Every day
in the morning
I check my
traps for
weasels and I
sell their hides
to Sears Roebuck
for 50 cents, $1.
Sometimes I buy
dresses or shoes
or make them
out of feed sack.
Every morning I
started the fire
at school and
holidays we
got sleds or
skis, then

we took them sliding. One night
sleeping we heard
something in our
cellar. My dad
took the 4-10 and
shot a badger with
big claws. Every
night we have
chamber pots to
use and washtubs
for toilets and
bathtub. No one
can imagine those
days long gone
in the dark.

My directions for the tenth-grade classes were slightly different. I wanted them to focus on one vignette from the life of Wilma or Parker and elaborate on it. I hoped the freedom to adapt a story in their own terms might appeal to the somewhat disinterested teenagers. Swanville sophomore Lisa L. rose to the occasion by capturing Parker's humor and cadence through the use of unusual line breaks and staccato pauses.

My routine in school was
flunk for two years, then pass to the next class.
I didn't deserve it
but that's the way my teacher was.
Soon to be divorced
she took her anger out on me.
I would answer a question right and
I would get embarrassed by her shouting
"Parker got something right"
to the entire classroom.
I got revenge by
shooting spitballs at her but
got punished by her,
took it in good humor
by laughing the whole time
my hair was being tugged.

Oral History Poems: A Two-Day Exercise

Step 1. Conduct the interview in the class. Good people to interview are retired teachers, coaches, grandparents, staff members, or friends of students' families. Someone over the age of fifty. Have an adult start the questions, and students chime in later. Students should jot down phrases or episodes that catch their fancy. Emphasize writing down exact phrases, to add a speaking quality to the poems. Writing a timeline on the board can help place public events such as World Wars, the Depression, etc.

Step 2. The next day, fill the board with favorite phrases from the interview. Discuss anything unclear or not understood. Comment on ways the person's childhood was different from today's.

Step 3. Read Jim Moore's poem and notice its listing of events in a memorable summer. Identify clues to childhood attitudes and behavior. Discuss the metaphor at the end, the comparison of leaves and gravestones. Encourage students to use a list shape and a startling metaphoric ending in fashioning their own poems.

Step 4. Vary moods and events and details to keep the poem lively. Tell the poem in the voice of the person interviewed. If they want, writers can enlarge on something only suggested, but the poem should stick as closely as possible to the speaker's words, trimming them and, if possible, creating a crisis. A crisis is almost always one event, different from repeated things of daily life.

Step 5. It helps if the teacher/writer creates a sample poem on the board, or the class can write a group sample poem to get started. Students may choose phrases from those gathered on the board or from their own notes. The ending, like Jim Moore's, should widen the scope of the poem by suggesting not only the passage of time, but also how looking back can reveal relationships among things otherwise considered discrete. Suggest some ways we mark time's passage: geese flying south, leaves turning, a face full of wrinkles, hands shaking with palsy. Then combine two elements and play around with words that evoke unexpected relationships: such as, "A drift of milkweed fluff whitening her hair."

On the final day of my residency, Kathy Detloff arranged for students to read their work at the Senior Center downtown. I had thought Swanville was flat, but as we bundled out onto Main Street, a hill sprang up behind the retirement home. Inside the Center's one-story brick building our audience of twenty-five waited around big windows. Murmurs of "That's Art and Jan's girl" or, "That's Clarence Anderson's grandson" greeted us. Wilma and Parker were present and, upon hearing the poems, took their newfound notoriety with good grace. Above and beyond which, something subtle emerged at the reception after the reading. To the students' surprise, the elders admitted there were things about the past they were happy to see go: among them, kerosene lamps and outhouses. The "old folk" were not simply nostalgic, as the students had supposed. "Make do with what you can't change" and "Enjoy what's better" characterized the attitude of much of rural Minnesota. Today's poetry needn't be nostalgic either, as the students' poems had shown.

II.

Some teachers think I'm great; a few never want to see me again. In the mid-1980s, when my residency work expanded to twelve weeks a year, principal Charles Askegard invited me to KMS (or Kerkhoven–Murdock–Sundburg), a small consolidated district about fifteen miles from the larger town of Willmar. Willmar is famous for its strike of eight women bank employees in 1978, chronicled in a documentary called *The Willmar 8*. Mr. Askegard suggested that I stay in Willmar at the Super 8 Motel opposite the train tracks because none of the KMS towns had any lodging. Such arrangements are common for residencies in very small towns. Even if motels exist, their indoor-outdoor carpeting often smells of hunters' beer; furthermore, eating in such small places can prove unnerving. I always seem to draw stares.

At Long Prairie, for instance, though I enjoyed scrumptious baked chicken and mashed potatoes in the only cafe that served dinner, several preschoolers stood up on their seats and proceeded to point at me. "Who's that?" they called. "Who's she staying with?" In an even smaller hamlet, farmers eyed me from under their feed caps while I ate lunch with the contact teacher. I soon realized that she and I were the only women in the diner. Earlier rural communities tended to treat their teachers like royalty. School-board presidents put them up, and churches vied for their voices in the choir. But the teachers were also held to strict account: they couldn't date, dance, or drink. If they managed to sneak off and do just that, they were put on probation or fired. Pure as a Madonna, retired if she became wedded to anything except knowledge, the rural schoolteacher might walk the weedy roads like a goddess, but she bore her employers' fear of outsiders and their admiration and suspicion of book learning. These days, when most female teachers in rural Minnesota have gone through school with everyone in their age group and are likely married to farmers, suspicion of outsiders is reserved for the likes of me. And I was wearing red cowboy boots with fringe. Not likely to inspire trust.

My first residency at KMS was an unusual two weeks: one spent at the elementary school in Murdock and another in the high school in Kerkoven, with occasional half days at tiny Norwegian Sundburg. With my usual schedule of only a week per school, I have many fewer sessions in a K–12 building. Happy to relax into KMS's generous schedule, I especially liked the afternoons when, swooping into Sundburg down a dip in the road, I felt as if I'd left the modern world behind and entered cozy Old Norway. Huge maples shaded porches spindled with spun-sugar. Surely courtly Mr. Askegard lived there. The *as* in his name danced with a Norwegian lilt. He explained that tiny Sundberg had retained its school because they wanted the freedom to teach a little Norwegian and to study Norwegian history and customs. Though I never partook of the school lunches, rumor had it that the cooks concocted meals of meatballs and potatoes, maybe even *lefse*, delicate potato pancakes dusted with sugar and rolled in jam.

My favorite teacher in the high school was Ruth Govig, whose husband was mayor of Kerkhoven, population 748, the largest of the three communities. Her eleventh-grade classroom was on the second floor of the old school, with tall windows and pools of sun on the wide maple floors. Built in 1904, and named after President Garfield, who was assassinated in 1881, its solid brick structure was a block off Main Street. Though I had always found some things wrong with the factory model of education which inspired this sort of architecture (where the teachers were compelled to act like foremen, regulating achievement through quotas and repetitive tasks), Ruth's building appealed to me with a kind of warped nostalgia. It stood foursquare in the center of town, as essential as any other kind of working establishment, and it didn't seem afraid of a certain kind of rigor.

By the time I had returned for my second residency with Ruth in 1998, however, the old high school was gone. "The new one is just west of town. Stay on Highway 12. You can't miss it." I had heard *that* before. But in this case her directions were as accurate as they were easy. During the fifteen-mile drive from Willmar, white feathers dusted the weeds at the roadside. Beyond was a series of low buildings, which I assumed sent birds to Willmar's main employer, Jennie-O's turkey-processing plants. Entering Kerkhoven, I crossed a railroad viaduct, slowed for the main street—railroad tracks and grain elevators on one side, storefronts on the other—then, on the periphery, sat the new school in a treeless swath, flat and amorphous. An American flag clacked in the prairie wind, and plovers piped in the grass. It was April and cold, but the grass was greening up.

As a rule, I am saddened by the demolition of fine old schools with their operatic windows, talkative staircases, and halls wide enough to thresh with a combine. New schools may operate with much the same philosophy as their forebears, yet they possess little of their older relatives' physical assertiveness. They hunker on the edge of small towns like shopping malls. Students arrive in school buses or cars that fill huge parking lots like tourist caravans. The buildings, with their vague shapes and lack of symmetry, level the character of their surroundings to a kind of no man's land. It's hard to tell which is the front or back door; multiple entrances snake out in thin erratic sidewalks. Often there are no windows. The building material is neutral, hard to identify, but probably concrete. As I walked toward KMS's new facility, across the prairie emptiness, I decided it was not so dissimilar from the turkey barns. Both serviceable, both containers for rearing live creatures, evocative of cleanliness over every other virtue. I hesitated to carry the comparison further.

Energetic, regal, and beautifully dressed, Ruth didn't seem fazed by the move. She helped orient me to the sprawling floor plan. All my classes would be down one corridor, she told me, and there, across the atrium, was a glassed-in media center where I could type up student work. Though the new corporate environment was elegant and streamlined, I worried that it symbolized a rejection or displacement of certain rural traditions. It's a cli-

ché of cultural analysis to bemoan the commercialization and homogeni-
zation of American culture. But perhaps not so obvious is the urbanization
of the K–12 curriculum: English texts with little from contemporary rural
writers, and the history of American agriculture generally taught only
through the Dust Bowl. Most school material, which does not speak to the
rural experience in all its change and complexity, betrays rural students to
the alienation and despair already smoldering in their communities. To
counterbalance this trend, I developed a group of exercises that would cultivate an appreciation of agrarian knowledge and rural wisdom. My first assignment at KMS asked students to write about things they learned *outside*
of school. The model was Kate Green's "Don't Make Your Life Too Beautiful," which celebrated the odd dislocations and accidents that make a place
unique:

> Don't fix the three-foot hole in the plaster
> over the stairway...
> You can look for hours at the pile
> of shingles your neighbor ripped off his roof
> and left to mold the green summer...
> Leave the old worn boots stacked in the hall,
> the rotten mattress in the flagstone basement.
> Live out your ecstasy on earth
> amid the flaking patio stones,
> the boarded up back door
> and the rusty car.[2]

What emerged from the students were poems built of aphorisms and
directives no city kid could have known. "Don't pee on an electric fence,"
wrote one boy. "Don't take a skunk out of your dog's mouth," wrote another. "Don't put your head down beside your dog when he's eating. Don't
tamper with baby snakes—the mother will come after you." Then, one
worthy of the Russian artist Chagall: "Goats can get up on roofs but can't
get down." Hmmm, I wondered as I handed back the papers with my red
exclamation marks, whose roof was it? "Don't shoot at baby gophers—the
mothers will attack you." Amazing ferocity of mothers. "Don't let your
cousin whirl your cat around by its tail. Don't stand behind a horse, or a
cow." Each line was a potential story. The absolute authority and uncanny
specificity of these lines impressed me with the students' knowledge of the

natural world. Since I had never tried this exercise with city kids, I had no basis for comparing country and city rascality. But Kate Green's poem had a city flavor to it, human detritus left to molder into its own kind of beauty, nothing like the frontier wildness of KMS seventh-graders.

The next year, on the advice of Ruth's replacement, Carol Thomton, I designed a similar exercise around the work of Minnesota poet Leo Dangel. One of Carol's favorite writers, Dangel writes of outhouse tipping, tractor driving, and pinochle playing with equal panache. I could tell at once that the voice of Dangel's irascible farmer Old Man Brunner—irreverent, bullish, oddly friendly—would strike a chord with the kids.

Old Man Brunner Spearing Carp on Wolf Creek

Early spring, rushing water,
he is out there, below the bridge
at a narrow channel, poised
with a pitchfork. He spears, pitches
huge carp onto the bank,
where they flop and buck until dust
cakes on their green scales.
Old Man Brunner will drive
around to neighbors,
giving away carp from a wet gunnysack.
This is Old Man Brunner's gift,
the flesh of the carp,
his way of almost giving himself,
and there are those who will accept.[3]

I was intrigued by this totemic character, slyly observed by the community, and by how he, in turn, judged his nit-picking observers with gentle irony. I thought the students would particularly enjoy Dangel's "How to Take a Walk." It poked gentle fun at a common occurrence, a farmer walking his fence line, carrying a shotgun. Yet the poem explored unexpected subtleties. Dangel's incisive strokes encouraged his rural readers to analyze a bit harder what they saw every day, to play the light of intelligence over the commonplace, and to let humor sharpen into truth, quietly but boldly. For students who may have felt that all great literature happened to people vastly different from themselves, Dangel offered a powerful corrective:

This is farming country,
The neighbors will believe
you are crazy
if you take a walk
just to think and be alone.
So carry a shotgun
and walk the fence line.
Pretend you are hunting
and your walking will not
arouse suspicion.
But don't forget
to load the shotgun.
They will know
if your gun is empty.
Stop occasionally.
Cock your head and listen
to the doves you never see.
Part the tall weeds
with your hand and inspect
the ground.
Sniff the air as a hunter would.
(That wonderful smell
of sweet clover is a bonus.)
Soon you will forget
the gun in your hands,
but remember, someone
may be watching.
If you hear beating wings
and see the bronze flash
of something flying up,
you will have to shoot it.[4]

I admired this poem for its savvy about farming culture: the insistence on work, and the suspicion of solitude or thought, and the spying of neighbors. I hoped it would gently insinuate the possibility of other forbidden enjoyable things, like poetry.

Dangel's humor seemed to invite the students to be themselves. They readily understood his allusions to the agrarian work ethic and the danger of appearing leisurely in "How to Take a Walk." "Do you experience this?"

I asked. Some of them called out, "Our *parents* do!" This made everyone laugh. "Think of the moments when your experience has gone against the grain. When you have been aware of experiencing something different, or choosing something different. The difference can be subtle, not huge; it can also be cloaked, not altogether obvious to the outsider."

The results, when I read them that night in the Super 8, were electric. Kaia W. captured an idiosyncratic expression that her grandpa was fond of:

> He's ready for church, dressed up real nice
> I grab the suspenders, pull back and release
> Namen-nakin-dooda, he says.

And Maggie S. wrote on a subject near and dear to my heart: being a newcomer in a tight-knit town.

Only a Friend

On the dock
feet in the water
waves splashing against the rocks
he grabbed the seaweed and threw it at me

On the dock
people yelling
we were talking and laughing
Then he stole my sweat shirt

On the dock
Jeff sitting on the paddle boats
I'm feeling out of place
my first day here

On the dock
he got me to open up
his sweet low voice giving the best advice I could get
no relationship potential at all

On the dock
feet in the water
waves splashing against the dock
he grabbed seaweed and threw it at me.

I liked the lapping repetition of "on the dock," and the gentle disclosure of the friendship that was not romantic, but in the end was more interesting than any amorous relationship.

Reading aloud the next day, the students showed more interest and respect for each other than they had before. Instead of scaling the peak of the exotic (provided by me) and worrying about showing off or failing at the game, they now were speaking with the laconic humor of their prairie experience, and doing just fine. The wide circle of poetry had expanded to include them.

Poems of Place and Character

Step 1. Two elements are crucial in Leo Dangel's poems: character and images of places. For brainstorming, therefore, start by having students draw a quick sketch of a person in an interior or exterior space. Some may emphasize one event, others a person with whom they had many experiences. The place can include a character's favorite chair or vehicle.

Step 2. Label the drawings. Who is in the drawing, what else do you see, where does this take place, when was it (occasion, season, age), why (the feelings, actions, favorite expressions associated with this person)?

Step 3. Selecting a small element in the drawing—the handlebars of a bike, or the shape of a flower—ask the magic question, "What else does it look like?" Write the comparison beside the thing in question. These comparisons may or may not make their way into the poems, but they suggest how poetry can involve transformation and surprise.

Step 4. Add a phrase about the place: "at Lake Elsie," "in the barn." And favorite quips, questions, songs, sayings of the person in the drawing.

Step 5. Choose a favorite phrase in the brainstorming, circle it, and use it as a repeated refrain in the poem. This could be a favorite saying of the person whose portrait you are writing, or it can be a comparison: "bike tire like a slice of orange." The repetition will link unrelated bits of memory with a songlike quality, and the refrain can be slightly changed to suggest developments in the poem.

III.

To city dwellers, rural America may seem as far away as the moon, or at least as foreign as a picture from an old issue of *Ideals,* that glossy magazine of rhymed nostalgia and landscapes with nothing taller than a silo and gold-green fields extending as far as the eye can see. Minnesota farmland still fits that mold, but farmers no longer plow with horses or raise six different crops. Since the mid-twentieth century, American agriculture has undergone a massive transformation.

Carol Thomton's brother, Jim Van Der Pol, was able to tell me about this first hand.[5] He and Carol grew up on a farm on the outskirts of Kerkhoven, which he and his family still work. As a boy, he helped his parents with their 320 acres of fertile "wet prairie" soil. They raised five or six crops and two or three forms of livestock: cattle, sheep, and chickens for sale and for personal consumption. "No self-respecting farmer would buy eggs in a store," Jim recalled. They had to be canny, self-reliant, and prepared to manage what the seasons, and their choices, dealt them. Though the family ran some fuel-powered machines, they did so only when the tractors and trucks made human work easier. In general, their rule was never to replace human workers. All of this began to change during World War II, when the U.S. Department of Agriculture started lobbying for the consolidation of farms, hoping to move agricultural workers off the land and into factories. Consolidation continued, even increased after the war, and simultaneously, many local wetlands were drained to increase tillable acreage. As a consequence, Jim and farmers like him currently farm every acre, compared to his parents, who worked only two-thirds of the total acreage. Increased farm size and huge machinery have also created a slow but steady drop in rural population. Since the 1960s, Jim reckoned, "we've lost about 90 percent of our farm population in this area." Bigger farms have meant fewer farm families. It stands to reason that since bigger machines work larger fields and it costs more to purchase a large farm machine than a house, farmers who want to stay in the game must buy out their neighbors. This consolidation of what were smaller family farms into larger family or, more likely, corporate farms has forced many farm workers into towns and from there into cities. At the same time, Jim pointed out, many former farmers have retired to town, living on Social Security or money from acreage they've sold.

As a kid, Jim shadowed his father. "You could find me if you found my dad and looked down. I was close to my twenties before I had a hero other than him. I wanted to unload hay and stock hay bales as fast as my dad could. It took me a while to beat the bull." In the 1950s and 1960s, farming wasn't particularly dangerous; Jim could be constantly underfoot, learning by observing and doing, and not endanger himself or his father. But that isn't true anymore. Today, the huge machines used on 1,000-acre farms are too dangerous and expensive to let anyone but an expert run and repair them. Moreover, the machines do almost all the work. "Contrary to the received wisdom," said Jim, "it's tough to be a boy in this society." By that, he meant that today few rural boys can work at learning how to farm. "The ag[riculture] teacher at our school gets requests from farm boys in October to camp out in the school shop. They don't want to go home," Jim reported. The collaboration of entire families in farming—wives and husbands, daughters and sons—has also decreased, because the machines are dangerous and difficult to operate. Farm girls may still run milking machines, but they usually don't drive combines. "Harvesting is a harrowing time, when huge machines reap, thresh, and bale as fast as the weather allows," Jim continued. There is no longer need for the strong, young arms of Jim's generation. "It's as if their families and community have told these boys, 'There's no place for you.' The farm economy does not include them." Their options after high school are either to get a factory job in the county seat or the Twin Cities suburbs, or to become a farmhand driving one of the huge combines.

Jim and his son Josh have resisted the dehumanization of agricultural expansion in favor of a return to older-style agriculture. They have shifted from "cropping to grazing," with more than half of their land in perennial grasses which they cut to feed and bed their cattle. "We are trying a new philosophy based on principles from the Amish," explained Jim. "Every time we consider acquiring machinery, we ask, 'Is it gonna replace people or enable people to do their work better?' Someday, I hope we will have a community that can ask, 'Will this machine replace my neighbor?'"

IV.

As I continued to work in rural towns—Hallock, population 1,100, on the eastern edge of glacial Lake Agassiz and twenty miles from Canada—I became more attuned not only to what characterized their similar pasts, but also to subtle redefinitions occurring from shifts in population and attitudes to the land. "When my husband was growing up here," "Charlie" Lindberg explained, "his dad hauled 25,000 gallons of fresh water from town out to the property. It had to last a year. Believe me, they took short showers!" Charlie, a media specialist at Kittson Central High School and my contact teacher for a one-week Hallock residency in 2003, had grown up in the Twin Cities. The week we'd been planning for over a year would celebrate rural history and land, including poems about abandoned farms, oral histories of Hallock old-timers, a driver's ed class that would produce "road odes," and a senior-class video documentary of the residency. But Charlie's perspective was on technology and social change. She talked about satellite imaging of farm fields; driving to Winnipeg, ninety miles away, for theater and concerts; and, in her husband's absence, selling crop futures over the Internet.

The first day of my residency, Sander Gustafson, born in 1920, paid a call to my ninth-grade class. He arrived for his oral history interview with a bale cutter, a bark trimmer, and a harness awl in tow, and proceeded to describe a brace of six horses his father had used for swathing and threshing. (Truth be told, if Mr. Gustafson had been twenty years younger, I'd have had a crush on him. With his sparkling blue eyes, craggy Scandinavian features, and slim build, he carried our hearts away in his Viking grip.) These days, he told us, in place of the horses, farmers invested in combines with air conditioning, radios, heat, even a TV. Each combine costs upward of $250,000 with prices rising—far more than *houses* in Hallock, which, I soon discovered, were going for as low as $22,000.

After Sander's visit, we rummaged through a series of photographs Charlie and her husband had taken of dilapidated farms in the area. Unlike my own collection, which portrayed idyllic images from an earlier era, Charlie's photos captured barn roofs depressed like swaybacked horses, weather-beaten houses with gaping windows and sagging porches, and overgrown grain bins from contemporary Hallock. Far from being bothered by these symbols of decay, the students seemed to get a kick out of identifying the whereabouts of each ruin. "You know about teenagers and empty houses and old barns?" Charlie whispered. For an instant I looked at her. Then I got it: prime real estate for drinking and making out.

One of the most striking poems to emerge from studying these images was "The Complainers." Blunt and ironic, the poem displayed a farm boy's knowledge of a barn and the work that it occasioned. I was touched by the thought that the barn itself might regret the loss of older farming styles that used many hands. Maybe the writer glimpsed his own obsolescence. Though this was a stretch, the poem's mixture of sympathy and harsh realism suggested a personal investment beyond either romantic nostalgia or an eagerness for the new.

The Complainers

I was once clean, says the
filthy concrete. I was once filled
with joy, says the empty stalls.
As I stand here, I wonder why
our owners abandoned us, says the
rotten support legs. The Petersons tended
their livestock in us and we protected
them through rough times.

Weathered and rotten, that's why they left
plus we are too small, too old, too weak
to stabilize, says the wise rafters.
We should just collapse and fade away.
There is no need for us, look at us,
we're empty, dirty, old, rotten, weathered and
all the windows are broken. As the breeze
rushes through, the door says, that's enough,
quit complaining. They are never coming back.
                        —Jason

Places Speak: An Exercise Based on Ted Kooser's "Abandoned Farmhouse"

The call and response of Ted Kooser's poem fleshes out the abandoned site by having its clues suggest characters and elements of a story:

> He was a big man, says the size of his shoes
> on a pile of broken dishes by the house ...
> Money was scarce, say the jars of plum preserves
> and canned tomatoes sealed in the cellar-hole ...
> Something went wrong, says the empty house
> in the weed-choked yard. Stones in the fields
> say he was not a farmer ...[6]

It is a simple matter to move from one element to another of an abandoned site, as the Hallock students did, and first list them, then return and imagine the events or sensations they suggest. The Hallock students used photographs of sites within their own county to spark recognitions. They also brought to bear their own experience of farming and the oral histories they had heard.

See my book *The Story in History: Writing Your Way into the American Experience* (Teachers & Writers Collaborative, 1992, pp. 29–39) for an extended version of this exercise.

All this talk of crumbling structures heightened the irony of our subsequent discussion with seniors about their class trip to Washington, DC, and New York City. The students told me they were stunned by the number of homeless people in Manhattan. Despite the ruined barns that we'd elegized, nobody in Hallock was homeless. On the contrary, homes stood empty. This helped explain the low housing prices, but it also indicated a loss of population. I didn't want to interrupt the seniors' New York stories with ruminations on the farm economy, but I thought that the plight of urban homeless mirrored the disenfranchisement occurring among rural people. The same way that farming with larger and larger acreages displaced smaller farmers, other U.S. jobs were being lost when companies outsourced or mechanized. It remains a disturbing trend.

With the seniors' foray into the larger world, our discussion about homelessness, and the techno-age measurement of soil moisture beamed by satellite onto a tractor cab's TV screen (couldn't the farmer simply step out and test the soil with his hands?), a reeling giddiness pushed me toward an exercise I would not have used with rural students before, thinking it too surreal. Based on Charles Simic's "Read Your Fate," the exercise asked young writers to make a progressive leap from local observations to more metaphoric and worldwide dislocation. In the poem, a familiar world of narrow street, one dog, a child, a big mirror, gradually narrows to two lovers who are loaded into an open truck. They travel on their sofa,

> Over a darkening plain,
> Some unknown Kansas or Nebraska ...

A storm boils up and the woman raises a red umbrella. Behind them, run the boy and dog

> As if after a rooster
> With its head chopped off.[7]

I emphasized how change could sometimes seem both dreamlike and shocking. Details become fixed in our minds because they have acquired the startling revelation of shock itself.

Following another inspiration, I built surprise into the writing process and adopted a collaborative, "pass-it-back" brainstorming technique, which results in a list to be used in drafting a poem. The students began the assignment by writing down a descriptive phrase about their neighborhood—all still recognizable and familiar. Then, they folded that statement down so it would not be seen, and passed their papers to the person behind them, who in turn was told to list a vehicle. This passing back continued in the scrambled-word game Mad Libs manner, with the following directives at each stage:

- name an activity
- name something glamorous
- describe a kind of weather
- choose a state in the Union
- name something happy
- describe a type of disintegration

By the end, the students had their own papers in their hands again. Using the wildly divergent list they had received to start their drafts, some students wrote poems ranging from the apocalyptic to the zany. A few captured the surreal energy of a foray into oblivion:

> The world is disappearing.
> Watching the neighbor's woods.
> Noticing a new pickup
> pulling into its driveway.
> A little girl hops out
> with bright gold chains
> hanging from around her neck.
> All of a sudden
> it was as if a hurricane
> made the girl fly away
> with her super-green
> umbrella.
> When I awoke,
> the woods were on fire
> and the state of Maine was no more.
> —Travis

Notes to Pass-It-Back/The World Is Disappearing

The best age level for this exercise is sixth grade and older. Younger students would probably take it into a fairy tale or a Harry Potter/ *Star Wars* kind of fantasy. Charles Simic's "Read Your Fate" poem gains its eerie and compelling quality by mixing the utterly commonplace with sudden twists. History is full of such unfoldings, gradual but ultimately frightening. It might not hurt to discuss things such as the Holocaust or environmental damage, that enlarge into horrors. Tornadoes from a great distance seem mere streaks at the horizon. Initially innocuous but slowly foreboding: this is the stuff of riveting literature. Comment on the power of such collaborative brainstorming; suggest to students that by bringing others into their creative process, they can free themselves from their own usual associations; and urge them to use a light touch as they link the various elements of the brainstorming into a narrative undoing.

Like many communally brainstormed poems, these had a special charm when read aloud. Students recognized their words in someone else's poem, and enjoyed seeing how they had been transformed, sliding toward surprising denouements. The teachers were pleased with the week's worth of writing and the public reading.

Farming, in this era of huge acreages, satellites, and chemicals, was a matter of tremendous risks. Poetry might cost nothing, but it required most of these students to experiment with a new form and then read their green attempts to their peers. Over the course of the week, the perception had shifted from poetry as razzle-dazzle (which rural communities could easily refuse to take seriously) to poetry as an expression of necessary creativity. Enmeshed with barn building and storytelling, poetry had acquired an honored place among the materials and methods farm families must cultivate to survive. The difference between citified poetry imported in textbooks and poetry locally made with materials at hand seemed particularly important where old-style farming with its closeness to animals and crops was being supplanted. With self-sufficient earthiness, the students teetered on the edge of their own oblivion. Some night they might walk into the barn for the last time and find poetry caught in its rafters.

NOTES

[1]James Moore, "That Summer, for Marijo," *25 Minnesota Poets #2* (Nodin Press, 1977, p. 194). Moore had gone to prison as a draft resister during the Vietnam War, as had his friend Fran Galt, who became my second husband. In 2005 Moore published his sixth volume of poetry, *Lightning at Dinner* (Graywolf Press).

[2]Kate Green, "Don't Make Your Life Too Beautiful," *If the World Is Running Out* (Holy Cow! Press, 1983, p. 62).

[3]Leo Dangel, "Old Man Brunner Spearing Carp on Wolf Creek," *Home from the Field* (Spoon River Poetry Press, 1997, p. 20).

[4]Dangel, "How to Take a Walk," ibid., p. 44.

[5]Phone interview with Jim Van Der Pol, 2002.

[6]Ted Kooser, "Abandoned Farmhouse." I originally read this poem in *A Geography of Poets* (Bantam Books, 1979, p. 228). Since my early acquaintance with Kooser's poetry, I've come to know him and his work better. This is especially delightful since he was appointed U.S. Poet Laureate in 2004.

[7]Charles Simic, "Read Your Fate." I encountered this poem first in *The New Yorker*. As I often do, I tore the poem out of the magazine, losing all but the date of the publication: 1993. Since then, I've encountered Simic's poetry in Carolyn Forche's magisterial anthology *Against Forgetting: Twentieth-Century Poetry of Witness* (W. W. Norton & Company, 1993). Simic's poems about his childhood experience of World War II in Yugoslavia and Italy led me to associate "Read Your Fate" with the Holocaust, but that remains an untested assumption.

CHAPTER TWO

From the Horn of Africa to St. Paul: Guiding ELL High-School Refugees from Fear to Personal Expression

I.

Gatekeepers, gun searches, food courts, and detention centers: if high schools represent what we offer immigrants, I am afraid of what these walled cities suggest. Yet within the fortress lie classrooms of exceptional promise, which sometimes become like paradise, like protected gardens. One of my favorites was Jane Sevald's ELL (English Language Learner) class at St. Paul's Como Senior High School. In the winter of 2002, she invited me to work with a group of refugee students from the Horn of Africa. Though I had taught other immigrant groups, notably the Hmong from the highlands of Laos, I knew little about these most recent Minnesotans, desert people from Somalia, Eritrea, and Ethiopia. It was surely one of life's ironies that people from the world's hottest spots kept being drawn to frigid Minnesota.

Before I presented an exercise to Jane's class, we agreed that I should visit as an involved observer, making myself familiar with the class as they became acquainted with me. Jane and her volunteer co-teacher Linda Kantner were exceptionally at ease with the students. Threats of "beating your heads in" and "calling your parents" made everyone laugh. Skating over the disorder of the students' lives, the teachers sought to supplant tears and terror with laughter.[1]

The class of fifteen students was unusually intimate for this era of budget cuts. But the school understood that smaller ELL classes made learning English easier and also encouraged trust. Though the class was small, its members represented vast, dislocated space and fractured time. As if the sun had risen, a young woman named Shumi, who is Oromo, lit up the room with tales of once-upon-a-time Christmas festivities in Ethiopia.[2] Shumi's father was Christian and her mother had converted to Christianity and learned to read. I remembered that an Ethiopian friend had described his own Christianity as descended from the Egyptian Coptic church, one of the earliest in the Christian diaspora. This suggested how closely North Africa was allied to countries and cultures around the Mediterranean, with Islamic and Christian elements existing side by side in many countries, as, for example, in Sicily. The moment Shumi paused, Dr. Ali Jama (Ph.D. in clinical chemistry from the University of Padua, Italy) turned and shook my hand. "Somalia: the land of perfume." The tall, limber school-community liaison flourished a patriotic bow. Fluent in English, Somali, and Italian (Italy had operated schools in Somalia, its former colony), Dr. Jama had once been a member of Somalia's educated elite. Now he carried the burden of better days with unusual grace.

From another corner, Hozan, a young man in high-top red sneakers, acknowledged my presence. During Saddam Hussein's genocidal war on the Kurds, Hozan had been forced out of Iraq to live first in Iran, then Turkey, and now the Upper Midwest. Later Jane and Linda shared their concerns about Hozan and his fellow students: as survivors of war and evacuation, they frequently suffered from post-traumatic stress syndrome (PTS) which left them fatigued, full of rage, hyperactive, or depressed. Not surprisingly, their schoolwork suffered, especially their personal writing.[3] Earlier in the year, Jane and Linda had tried personal topics with the students, such as descriptions of their names, or of places and people they remembered from home. The topics had caused distress and confusion. Personal history was too painful to write about. Trying a more neutral approach, Jane and Linda had recently assigned a five-paragraph essay about a photo Jane had found on the Internet. I was intrigued to see how the teachers would present this standard high-school assignment—the five-paragraph essay—to students whose lives were a far cry from linear. A teasing idea suggested itself: when my turn came to teach the class, I would choose poetry. Poetry cut through linear logic and went straight to the heart of memory and chaos. Though the students might balk, perhaps poetry's oblique circuit of craft and feeling would win them over.

Since writing from photos has been one of my favorite poetry-writing activities, I was curious to see how Jane and Linda would develop the photo assignment. Each student had a copy of the same photo, and for several days as a class they had worked on vocabulary, an essential for ELL students. As I cruised the room, looking over their shoulders, I spotted the photo subject of their essays: a young woman in high heels and a white dress knelt beside a roadster with a flat tire. The image seemed innocuous, even banal. Would it elicit much interest? Then Sildavine, a shy student from Cambodia, pointed to the bottom of the photo: small red crabs swarmed like a tide across the asphalt. I would have missed them entirely without her help. Sildavine had written, "Running over the crabs had caused her tire to puncture." More literate than most of the East Africans who had spent years in Kenyan refugee camps, Sildavine had attended college in Cambodia.

"Why don't you describe the crabs some more," I suggested. "What color are they?" She promptly answered, "Red." "What do they look like?" I asked, trying to lead her to the next associative step. "The crabs look like walking flowers," she wrote. I was thrilled with the lovely image. Laughter and loud voices broke into our conversation. Some young Somali men at the back of the room were cutting up, nothing at all like the shy, deferential Hmong immigrants with whom I had worked in the past. I soon discovered, however, that these East African young men were not all gleeful. In one of their earlier drafts, words and phrases flew around like sharp, deadly shrapnel. Now, every sentence in Ramzy's first paragraph veered off in a different direction.

"How old do you think she is?" Ramzy asked about the young woman in the photograph. Taken by surprise, I hesitated, realizing that many of these students were in their twenties, older than most high school students. "Twenty-five?" I guessed. The other young men giggled; I suspected they had been talking about flirting with her. Yet Ramzy had written nothing lighthearted; instead he had created a brutal, sexual scenario in which she was beaten by an abusive husband and was now trying to escape. Was this fearsome imagination part of the PTS Linda and Jane had warned me about? Ramzy had found brutality in a situation that to me appeared merely frustrating. His words and ideas also jumped around as if it were impossible to create linear order in the woman's nightmarish predicament. Did he experience his own life this way? Living for months or years on the run, many of these young adults had been separated from everyone they knew. It was an unusual youth, like Dr. Jama's son Hassan, whose parents had accompanied him or her to safety.

The undercurrent of sexuality among the young men was impossible to ignore. Not wanting to address it directly, I decided to engage Ramzy in simple questions and answers. I also responded a bit to his flirtatious demeanor. Acting the damsel in distress, I smiled. "You won't believe this," I said, "but I have never changed a tire. Tell me how to do it." He straightened up and out of his mouth came words like "lug nuts" and "tire irons." Could it have been that he had planned to rescue the stranded heroine all along? As the common laughter died away, Ramzy bent over his paper and began to write graciously to the lovely lady, describing the steps necessary for her to change the tire herself.

This little shift away from the heroic rescue of a damsel to helping her take care of herself suggested how we teachers presented ourselves: as modern American feminists. Now, as I met a handful of young women who wore the traditional Muslim hijabs (derived from the Arabic word *hajaba*, meaning to cover or conceal), I depended on Jane and Linda to help me decipher East African Muslim gender roles. *Hijab* in Somalia, *aba* in Saudi Arabia—these terms designated the flowing garments worn by traditional Muslim women. I had seen women dressed in these usually dark robes on Twin Cities streets and now, as I approached the veiled young women in Jane and Linda's class, my initial impression was that the students were as shy and retiring as their outer covering, not eager to speak up in class or to converse one on one about their writing.

One day when I was not in class, two girls in full hijabs presented Jane with an Internet poem supporting veiling. Veiling was evidence of a woman's dedication to Allah, the poem said. Though many non-Muslim Americans interpreted hijab as a sign of women's submissiveness to male domination, it actually freed the wearer to claim her own power, the poem explained. Hijab announced a woman's pride in being Muslim and her control of her own sexuality. Jane had courteously read the poem and praised the students' resourcefulness in finding it, but a few days later when she, Linda, and I met for coffee, she kidded that the girls were trying to convert her. The Internet poem had prompted one of several discussions among the girls and Jane about the advantages of hijab. The fact that the students had again taken up the issue of dress with Jane suggested that they wanted her to understand hijab so she could wear it and protect herself as they did.

Underneath Jane's wry humor, I suspected, lay the philosophy that religion should be kept separate from public education. As veterans of the American feminist movement, Jane, Linda, and I also had personal experience with constraining garments and women's absence in workplace and politics. It was hard for us not to worry that the hijab might interfere with the students' range of movement, or more subtly discourage their active public participation. But Jane, Linda, and I never challenged the students' choice of attire or, certainly, their religious beliefs.

In contrast to the shy behavior of some young women who wore hijabs in class was the boisterous behavior of others who combined Muslim veils with standard American jeans and sweaters. They sounded like loud, street-smart urban teenagers, perhaps more angry than most, but using the same slang and attitudes as American teens. Occasionally I wondered if their rapid adjustment had created stress above and beyond the obvious dislocation of their recent immigration. Then again, perhaps their choice of more American-style clothes had freed them to speak out. Like so many things, it seemed that wearing hijab was deeply individual to the wearer, and its meaning could not be generalized.

In another conversation, Jane and Linda mentioned that East African students often came to the United States alone or with parental surrogates. Sometimes the students slept on relatives' couches in the Twin Cities and were abruptly shifted from one house to another. As with many other immigrant groups before them, their hardships continued after they landed in America.

In free moments, I reflected back to other teaching I'd done with earlier immigrant populations, largely Southeast Asians. Like the East African students, most of the Southeast Asian immigrants had escaped a kind of civil war. The Hmong had run through the Laotian jungle and crossed the dangerous Mekong River to wait in Thai refugee camps for immigration visas. (From 2004 to 2006, the last groups would receive permission to settle in the United States.) In the camps, few of them received much formal education. The Hmong language had not been written down until the 1950s, when missionaries had created an orthography to help the people read the Bible. Yet, as a group, the Southeast Asians had made excellent ESL students. (ESL: English as a Second Language, an earlier designation for what was now called ELL or English Language Learner.) The Hmong and other Southeast Asians were quiet, deferential to elders, appreciative, and hard-working; they hadn't shown the effects of PTS in class as markedly as did some of the African refugee students I was getting to know at Como High. In the late 1980s, I had read that recently arrived Hmong men sometimes died suddenly in their sleep. And I had seen a play written by Hmong immigrant students about their uprooting and the tension that occurred in families as young people acquired English and wanted the greater freedom of American dating and relative independence from parental control. Now as I thought back to the classes I had taught with Hmong students, I concluded that the Hmong did indeed manifest the trauma of war and dislocation—how could they help but be deeply affected? Their manner of showing this trauma, however, differed from that of the refugees from East Africa, evidence of vast differences in their original cultures.

Working in St. Paul's Harding High School during the late 1980s, ESL teacher Darlene Kunze and I had developed a writing process for her entry-level ESL students. We began by asking them to draw familiar objects from home. My rationale was simple: I had observed the skill with which these students could draw; drawing a familiar object or room or person brought them into immediate contact with a subject. Next, we asked them to conduct English question-and-answer sessions about their drawings. First they spoke their questions and answers, because their speaking skills were stronger than their written. Then they wrote down their questions and answers. Choosing one of our own personal objects, Darlene and I had modeled the process of questions and answers. The students followed suit. The process had proved an excellent way to teach new words and concepts and to enhance the sense of writing as developing out of speech. This was particularly effective for people from a largely oral culture, like the Hmong. The classes had helped Darlene and me turn our Q&A into short essays of one to three paragraphs, which were written on the board. Finally the students had been ready to write their own short essays. They told stories of treasured objects such as carved vases or bows and arrows, their drawings displaying the skill which had also fashioned these objects. Other students had recalled a room from home, the birth of a sibling, or, most poignantly and unimaginably, a grandmother whom the family had been forced to leave on the trail.

There had been a few unexpected glitches, but on reflection these glitches were precisely where Darlene and I had stumbled and learned the most. For instance, the Hmong students would not draw or write about anyone in their extended families who was dead. (I had no idea if such prohibitions extended to world figures such as Ho Chi Minh or George Washington.) For the Hmong, the dead retain considerable power over the living. If angered, disrespected, or annoyed, the dead can cause illness or disaster. Immediately, Darlene and I realized that we were teetering on the edge of a cultural abyss. On one side stood the Western dead, remote and powerless, but memorialized in language and imagery; on the other gathered the still vital Hmong dead, quite prickly about the way they were portrayed. To the students, we suggested that they write not about dead grandfathers but about living mothers or the water buffalo who had served the family in Laos.

Also unexpected was the intense difficulty that the students had with the tasks. They were, after all, trying to learn three or four new skills at once: to read and write for the first time, and to do so in a foreign language. Moreover, they were moving from a largely oral culture, especially the Hmong, to a highly literate one. An eloquent oral narrative in the Hmong culture would frequently feature repetition (much like the role of a refrain in song or of incantation in poetry). Later I would learn that Somali poetry, also largely oral, declaimed elaborate invocations to friends who became the poet's audience. Such narrative structures could hardly be corrected with a red pen; in fact, it was questionable if they should be corrected at all.

II.

When my turn came to lead Jane's ELL class in a poetry lesson, I remembered Ramzy's nightmarish story about the young lady, and decided to avoid any potentially vulnerable or dangerous topics. Instead, I ventured to introduce Tu Fu's "Written on the Wall at Chang's Hermitage," a poem whose subject was at a temporal and spatial remove from the students. The eighth-century Chinese poet would provide an easy-to-follow, evocative model, the voice of a fellow wanderer. Like the students, Tu Fu had spent part of his life on the move, leaving a diplomatic post for a life of river boating, a life he described as sometimes full of raucous carousing and sometimes filled with lonely drifting. Between these extremes, he wrote appealing, concise poems about weather and the seasons. In "Written on the Wall at Chang's Hermitage," the season begins with a broad stroke: "It is spring in the mountains," but then Tu Fu introduces the first of many subtle gradients to fill in the scene. The "sound of chopping wood" suggests that fires are still needed; this is early spring, not almost summer. There is still snow on the trail. As the traveler enters, the scene reveals itself in small details, fragmented in a way that I hoped the students might recognize from their own introductions to new locales, yet filtered through Tu Fu's single sensibility, and thus aspiring to be whole.

> It is Spring in the mountains.
> I come alone seeking you.
> The sound of chopping wood echoes
> Between the silent peaks.
> The streams are still icy.
> There is snow on the trail.
> At sunset I reach your grove
> In the stony mountain pass.
> You want nothing, although at night
> You can see the aura of gold
> And silver ore all around you.
> You have learned to be gentle
> As the mountain deer you have tamed.
> The way back forgotten, hidden
> Away, I become like you,
> An empty boat, floating, adrift.
> —Tu Fu[4]

Though it was tempting to dive right in, I had to be patient. Vocabulary came first. It was interesting to consider that these mainly East African students were learning English via the translation of a Chinese poem.

Kenneth Rexroth's supremely masterful translation went down so easily that no one questioned it. Each language has its own manners, as the students would soon learn, and the Rexroth translation was a particularly effective poem in American English. Perhaps discovering that we could enjoy a poem written originally in a language none of us knew might also free the students to appreciate their own quirky responses as they learned new English words. "Pass," a narrow way between mountains, was definitely new to them. As were the words "aura" and "ore." "Tamed," once they understood the concept, was easy. "Adrift" was a stumbling block. Sometimes a little etymology helps: First "drift," as in "driftwood," and then the slang phrase, "Get my drift?" Finally they grasped "adrift," with its hint of laxness, loosening, getting lost.

When I came to class the next day, the students clamored to read Tu Fu's poem aloud. Half the period was gone before I realized that what had appeared to be eagerness was actually a form of stalling. The students didn't want to write: their behavior sometimes demanded interpretation as nuanced and prickly as new words. As I thought about the students' reluctance to write, I remembered my own attempt to learn Italian: reading in a foreign language is much easier than writing. In reading, unfamiliar words are often resolved by their context. Choices of subject matter, vocabulary, grammar, and style have all been made for us. But in writing we must select and arrange, try to mold complex ideas with our limited second-language competence. Frustration was inevitable. Writing, for Jane's students, no doubt also reminded them of their changed lives and torn pasts. They could read without undue distress about someone else's troubles (especially through the distant lens of a foreign language), but writing their own lines tore at their sleeves. Shumi, for instance, had come to the U.S. without her husband of a few months because her name, not his, had been drawn from the immigration lottery. Lamenting this to Linda and Jane, she gained solace, but if she were to write this across an empty page, she might flounder, alone in a solitary struggle.

For now, we would forget writing, I decided, remembering my long-ago process with the Hmong students. We would draw instead. Drawing was, after all, integral to Chinese writing and poetry; I felt quite natural asking the class to sketch a season. Not just any season, but spring, winter, fall, summer in a particular landscape. Here I was calling on poetry's circuitous craft to shake loose the students' memories of plants, breezes, waterfowl, gurgling water. Maybe if the class drew specific landscapes, they would unlock their memories and suffuse their poems with feeling. It was worth a try. "Tell the truth but tell it slant," Emily Dickinson had suggested. "Success in circuit lies." Maybe nature's leaf would waft them into personal territory before they knew it. For Alcides the particular landscape was a beach; for Ali too. "What ocean is it?" I asked Ali. "The Indian Ocean." I was moved at the mention of that august and distant body of water, the thought that an ocean I had never seen was present in the classroom. Sildavine rendered a mountain valley with palm trees shading small houses on stilts. She had done exactly what I had not dared suggest: she had drawn an image of home.

When Ramzy found a brown marker, he drew close-growing trees with dense interwoven branches, almost a bramble. Birds of purple and gray darted among the branches. Two young women in full hijabs drew elaborate variegated leaves that filled their papers. The drawings were reminiscent of Audubon's botanical sketches. Had they misunderstood my instructions to draw particular landscapes? Strict Muslim tradition forbade art-making except for purposes of identification or education. At the time when the Prophet Mohammed had received his religious revelation, hundreds of idols were worshipped. Allah taught Mohammed that this was a great sin. Since then, making images of humans or animals had become, for traditional Muslims, a defacement of divine law, for which they would be punished on the day of judgment. This was not so different from fundamentalist Christian prohibitions in earlier eras against dancing or the theater.[5]

Since we were drawing for educational purposes, no one overtly objected. As the momentum grew, I ventured a transition. I asked Ramzy what his tree trunks "looked like." "A fence," he said. Meanwhile, Sildavine was rifling the pages of her Khmer/English dictionary for a word to describe her palm. "Fan," she wrote beside her tree. Sildavine, born poet. "Now that we've got some nouns, could you add a verb to your comparison?" Alcides added the word "rise": "The mountain rises sharp as a knife."

While I was reveling in the response, Jane and Linda were struggling with some disruptive students in the back of the class. A girl I'll call Washti thought the exercise was "dumb" and refused to continue. Her words were accompanied by a fusillade of flung pencils and dropped books, the behavior of a much younger child. I couldn't afford to be disappointed or hurt: this is the nature of teaching. Interruption, rejection. There was only one tack to take: interrupt the interruption. "Why don't you read us what *you've* written."

> It's summer on the beach.
> The clouds are faces of people that
> You cared about.

There it was, the metaphor for pain which many students tried to avoid. Were the faces those of the dead or lost? No way of knowing. After her brief outcry, Washti quieted down and seemed to become a part of the group who had heard her.

As they resumed their writing, I urged the students to follow Tu Fu's example and use only a few details in each line. The poems they created were not all stunning. Some limped along, unable to find a rhythm. Others cut short, or dragged. I liked especially Sildavine's poem.

> It is spring in the morning
> All alone I walk looking for you
> The sound of birds and waterfalls makes interesting music
> Nature is still green
> The water is cool on my feet
> This morning, a palm tree blows like a fan
> The sky is holding houses in its hands and the trees are
> > blowing in the clouds.
> Beautiful green nature makes my heart joyful like flowers
> > getting water.

Ramzy's poem was also remarkable. We teachers said, "This is the day Ramzy learned 'purple.'" In his poem, purple mountains soared over the forest, and confusion and violence were limited to closed windows and confusing bird calls.

> It is winter in the forest.
> All alone I walk inside the forest.
> The singing of birds is in the forest.

The sounds of birds confuse me.
The birds sometimes are like purple mountains soaring over
the forest.
Tree trunks are like windows closed in the forest.
The forest and the people make me happy, like my
girlfriend.

In the midst of the exercise, Hozan of the red high-top tennis shoes raised his hand: "But who are we bringing with us into this land?" He remembered the hermit from the title of Tu Fu's poem. "Can I bring anyone I want? Can my wife come into this land?"

Journey through a Landscape Poem Exercise

(Short, one-day version for English speakers)

Step 1. Discuss Tu Fu and the similarity of his poem to haiku: it contains references to nature and to the season. Have students read it aloud, each person reading one line, to emphasize the completeness of each line and to enjoy a medley of voices.

Step 2. Identify the season as early spring: snow on the trail, the sound of chopping wood. Notice that each line delivers an element of sense experience or narration. Discuss Chang as a moral touchstone: he wants nothing (a double idea: he asks for nothing and lacks nothing, having enough). Gold and silver ore suggest the royal court which Chang, like Tu Fu, probably left. Ask what character traits are necessary for taming a wild deer. Answers: patience; attention to the animal's habits; persistence; and quiet, calm action. Ask students to consider the ending: "What would it feel like for your life to be this empty, this adrift?" Contraries come to mind: carefree, scary, willing to go with the flow, having no idea where you'll end up.

Step 3. Brainstorm a place and a guide. Students select a landscape after listing different kinds: desert, beach, valley, forest, prairie. They select a specific season—early spring, late summer, midwinter—after discussing elements of climate and weather, behavior of birds, trees, plants, clouds, wind, rain and snow, etc. Students list evidence of the season. They also imagine a person or animal they might encounter who, like Chang, would have traits from which they could learn. The place itself could be a teacher.

Step 4. Draft. Ask students to use the simple scheme of Tu Fu's poem, limiting the information in each line to one or two simple elements. Remind them of the three main "acts" of the poem: setting the scene and season; encountering a person, animal, etc., whose qualities initiate a change in the visitor; then describing the change in a metaphor. Encourage the writers to look within themselves for important lessons they have learned. The ending metaphor should be based on nature. It can be straightforward as in the ELL students' poems: "I am as happy or as natural as flowing water, etc." Or more ambiguous and complex as in Tu Fu's poem.

III.

Jane's classroom had the capacity to become a paradise of sorts, but the minute the students stepped outside, they entered the crowded hallways of the high school, a situation rife with embarrassments. Embarrassment: a potent high-school emotion, and one that I decided to draw upon for our next writing assignment—specifically, embarrassing situations in the lunchroom. It turned out to be an inspired choice. Though Jane's students had adjusted since entering school in September, the huge lunchroom at Como High remained a challenge. There they stood out among the crowds of English-gabbing, American-style teenagers. Not to mention the fact that the food smelled awful, and eating pork or pork sausage—a favorite topping on pizza—was against the Muslim creed.

It was mid-March. Cold, snow, and darkness had conspired to wear us all down. Ramzy of the purple birds hadn't come to class for a month; word was that he had dropped out of school. Many of the students had full-time jobs as janitorial workers at a casino in a distant suburb. With late-night bus rides compounded by the school bell ringing at 7:15 A.M., it was no wonder that many students rested their heads on their desks during class. Despite this, the students' dedication to the writing class was astonishing. Lunchroom embarrassment might be just the topic they needed to help vent larger frustrations. It also offered them a chance to reflect on how far they'd come. In their narratives, they could explore the initial fears of a newcomer from the vantage point of a seasoned veteran. Or, so I thought...

"I pointed at the pizza," wrote one of the young ladies in a hijab. "'Pork?' I asked the lunch lady. She took the pieces of pepperoni off, but I still couldn't eat it; we're not supposed to eat anything that pork has touched. I didn't know how to say that to the lady. She wanted to give me that pizza." Struck by the delicacy of this situation, I imagined the cafeteria staff trying to accommodate the student's need, and the student's difficulty with English forcing her to take something she could not eat. Embarrassment was only one of many emotions the lunchroom aroused. Dr. Jama's son Hassan brushed aside food embarrassment and went immediately to cross-cultural romance. He wrote about meeting a large beautiful girl in the lunchroom; later they went to the movies, but when he refused to introduce her to his parents, she dumped him. Such a meeting probably meant a far more serious step to him than it did to her. She might have been simply curious to inspect Muslim parents; he might have feared pledging a troth.

Another student, a girl who wore a full hijab, wrote about her former Koranic studies in Somalia: everything in her class had been orderly and serene. She did not mention Como High and the lunchroom at all. This was another hint that wrapping oneself in traditional Muslim garb soothed and protected some of the Muslim girls.

Alcides approached his lunchroom story under the protection of a metaphor.

> It was September 5, 2000, 11:35 A.M., and the bell rang. It was my first time for lunch. ... It was like a zoo inside, there were many kinds of animals like monkeys, lions, and wild dogs, and some cougars too. I walked down a corridor between Martians. It was so different to me to talk to them. [He bought unfamiliar food; paid $1.50.]
>
> I did not know where to sit, I was afraid of those same animals like monkeys, but I was not afraid of the blond girl that was there. I took a seat next to the cashier and there I sat for all my first year in Como High. It was difficult for me to meet somebody like the blond girl because I did not speak English.
>
> Now I feel like a person living in the jungle. ... It was my life to adjust to this jungle. So now I feel like an American person.

Alcides' extended zoo metaphor lent distance and literary style to his embarrassed uncertainty. I was touched by his admission that he had sat the entire year beside the cashier. At the end, Alcides did not conquer the jungle; rather he made peace with it. He had learned to "feel like an American person." Did this phrasing result from his linguistic awkwardness, or did it describe a complex psychological revelation? In order to assimilate, had he felt it necessary to assume a nation-sized identity?

Notes on Embarrassing Moments:
Short Memoir Essay Exercise

Step 1. Select a model that guides students in writing a sketch of their embarrassing moments. Our lunchroom model was a student essay found on the Internet. In this funny incident, a young woman was just about to drink a carton of milk when Mr. Beautiful spoke to her. She sputtered and the milk splattered all over her. The essay ended:

> I don't understand what happened to me! I decided I would just sit quietly and watch everyone else eat. Being a little hungry was a lot better than acting like a fool. As Mr. Beautiful talked I could feel my heart racing and my palms were cold and clammy!

With other students I have used segments from Stephen King's novella "The Body," which is the basis for the popular movie *Stand by Me*.[6] Students first write the skeleton of an embarrassing moment. With Jane's ELL class at Como High, the students first drew scenes of embarrassing moments, labeled them, and finally wrote about the drawings. I often read my prose poem called "Roman Nose," about being embarrassed in junior high. Teacher stories can be good models.

Step 2. To work on expanding their initial drafts, we discuss flashbacks as a narrative technique to give complication and depth to an incident. Flashbacks are keyed into the narrative through a "flash" of connection, a word or scent or taste, etc., that sparks a memory. The embarrassing-moment flashbacks sent the students to earlier moments of frustration or funny embarrassment, which they then wrote into their stories. (Note: I did not use this with the Como students.)

Step 3. Enlarge with comparisons and exaggeration. Stephen King's humorous, empathetic story of junior-high boys concludes with their discovery of a body killed by a train. This discovery is expressed by a series of negatives about what the body will never do again. "The kid wasn't going to get up in the morning anymore or get the runs from eating too many apples or catch poison ivy or wear out the eraser on the end of his Ticonderoga No. 2 during a hard math test." And so on, in roiling negatives, evoking everything from a "big glurt of cheap Halloween candy" to the negative side of a battery. Using this technique with their embarrassing moments, students could write that this moment was worse than, for example, flushing a toilet and being splattered with the water, getting your tongue stuck to a frozen door handle, having your pants split at a football game with everybody watching.

Step 4. Put some sort of resolution on the crisis of embarrassment. For some, this means moving ahead into the future and indicating what changes resulted from the embarrassment. For others, staying in the moment itself and intensifying its meaning is resolution enough. At the end of my "Roman Nose" poem, I went to the dark windows where outside nothing but the dark water was a friend. In a Cambodian student's prose piece, he explained how he changed his embarrassing name to one closer to American equivalents.

IV.

With spring came longer hours of sunlight. Alcides stayed late in Jane's class to talk about writing. "Don't you want to finish your footstool?" Jane urged, fearing that he would be late for his woodworking class.

"I want to learn how to write a love poem," he insisted. Alcides was Hmong, but had grown up in Argentina, with its Latin openness. He and many of the East African young men talked openly about women and marriage, but the Muslim young women in full hijabs shied away from the topic. A few of their counterparts who wore only headscarves reacted more like some American teens, thrilled by the drama and excitement of dating. They might take to writing love poems, I thought, but what about their more conservative sisters? Was romance a forbidden topic for them? Jane and Dr. Jama commented that within a Muslim family, girls were particularly sheltered, allowed to marry only Muslim men. Boys had more freedom, in many countries being allowed to marry Muslim, Christian, or Jewish girls. Within the sometimes polygamous Muslim family, a Western-style romance of two love partners would have to proceed circuitously, jealously guarded from the stakes others might have in it.

Jane, Linda, and I decided to celebrate different kinds of love, platonic and romantic. We would offer the students love of home, parents, nature, friends, even spiritual love, along with the celebration of a beloved's beauty. A search for Muslim poetry netted a smattering of works, but none from Somalia. Somali poetry was largely oral, I soon learned, transmitted through memorization. (See Chapter Five for a fuller discussion of this.) On the Web, I did find some poetry from Ancient Egypt and a number of translations from the thirteenth-century Persian poet Jalalludin Rumi, a Sufi Muslim mystic, who is very popular in the United States. Friends who read the mystics of Persia and India—Rumi, Hafiz, Kabir, Mirabai—find the poets' ecstatic descriptions of spiritual love lift them outside more ritualized or theological approaches to the divine, into a fund of universal experience. Even in Minnesota, land of Lutheran devotion, Rumi (along with Dr. Martin Luther King, Jr.) was quoted on a Duluth memorial to three African Americans lynched in the 1920s.

> We are the mirror as well as the face in it.
> We are tasting the taste this minute of eternity.
> We are pain and what cures pain.
> We are the sweet, cold water and the jar that pours.[7]

Rumi's love poems appealed to the students immediately; they enjoyed knowing that many Americans reveled in his words, which in the following poem summoned his readers (the listening "lovers") to begin a new life. This Rumi poem was more about pilgrimage than romantic longing, as Rumi urged his lovers to begin a trek toward spiritual insight. It didn't hurt that the conveyances included camels and caravans.

Lovers

> O Lovers, Lovers, it is time
> to set out from the world.
> I hear a drum in my soul's ear
> coming from the depths of the stars.
>
> Our camel driver is at work;
> the caravan is being readied.
> He asks that we forgive him
> for the disturbance he has caused us,
> he asks why we travelers are asleep.
>
> Everywhere the murmur of departure;

the stars, like candles,
thrust at us from behind blue veils,
and as if to make the invisible plain,
a wondrous people have come forth.[8]

As a counterpoint to Rumi, I selected William Shakespeare's Sonnet CXXX, "My mistress' eyes are nothing like the sun." Far from ecstatic, its crabby assertiveness grabbed the students immediately. I was surprised by how excited they were to read it aloud, again and again. Maybe its contrariness appealed to them, capturing the way they chafed at standards and judgments that penned them in or out. Shakespeare stood at the pinnacle of classic English poetry, I told them, emphasizing that they were reading the best of our tradition as well as the best of their own. I also hoped that following Shakespeare's model of repeated comparisons would help the students shape their own confused thickets toward some form of self-understanding. It was surprising to find that they were at ease with Shakespeare's archaic language, or rather, that it seemed no more difficult to them than any other unfamiliar English lines.

My mistress' eyes are nothing like the sun;
Coral is far more red than her lips' red;
If snow be white, why then her breasts are dun;
If hairs be wires, black wires grow on her head.
I have seen roses damask'd, red and white,
But no such roses see I in her cheeks;
And in some perfumes is there more delight
Than in the breath that from my mistress reeks.
I love to hear her speak, yet well I know
That music hath a far more pleasing sound;
I grant I never saw a goddess go;
My mistress, when she walks, treads on the ground:
    And yet, by heaven, I think my love as rare
    As any she belied with false compare.[9]

"He doesn't like the way his lady looks," Washti called out. We laughed and did not discuss sonnet structure or difficult phrases. Instead we launched immediately into comparing facial features with natural elements. By this time in the year, the students were thoroughly comfortable making comparisons. "Eyes like shining stars," set the norm; Sildavine's "mouth like a bird cheeping" opened the way to fresh comparisons. When we turned to negative ones, many students went hog wild, as if venting frustration on this putative lover gave them great pleasure. "A lover's neck?" I asked, and Ramzy suggested, "A giraffe." Outlandish to me, but probably not to him. Somalia and Kenya were full of strolling long-necks. Washti used garbage for the smell of her lover's breath. I chose dirty socks.

The love poems, written the next day, didn't always parse with perfect English grammar. Some students almost never used prepositions; others had trouble with verb tenses. But all the poems had sharp contrasts and looked like poems. Given Shakespeare's anti-ideal love, it wasn't surprising that some of the students' love poems were almost insults. Hozan wrote:

> My lover's eyes don't sparkle like the stars, they are dust.
> Her mouth doesn't taste like sweet apples, it tastes like old
>   nasty apples.
> Her neck is not strong like a tree, it is like a long stick that can
>   be broken easily.
> The smell of her skin and breath does not smell like fresh air,
>   it smells like dirty socks.
> The sound of her voice isn't like the waterfall's, it is like the
>   sound of a machine gun.

When Hozan read "machine gun," the class gasped. It was rare for the students to mention the wars that many had experienced. I remembered that Hozan had wanted a lover to accompany him into his Tu Fu landscape. Now a fictional lover metaphorically shot him. Was he simply following the anti-ideal assignment or had the formula struck a chord of distress? I imagined that finding love in a new land could cause intense anxiety.

In her poem, Hinda sounded the note of a street-smart American girl, a response which fit her outspoken, ironic demeanor. She did not wear a protective veil but, it seemed to me, she warded off romance by portraying it as decidedly unpleasant:

> My lover's eyes are brown like chocolate
> But not as sweet
> . . . .
> His voice sounds like a lion's roar and his breath smells like a
>   skunk
> I hope the lover in this poem doesn't end up with me.

This was one of the most accomplished sassy poems, and not the only one written by a girl. I wondered if Hinda had responded to American feminism with exaggerated harshness. Not knowing her well, I also wondered if she had picked up some American street talk which now spilled out in her poem. I was glad to see that she could discard the unpleasant lover, feeling no duty to keep him for herself. But that was the feminist in me. The mother in me hoped that someday she would find someone whom she found appealing.

There were sweet love poems, not surprisingly from Alcides, the eager Latin lover, who wrote an adoring song to "My Lover":

> My lover's eyes are like the intense
> > Days of spring
> . . . .
> Her skin is like gold and very soft
> > When I touch her
> Her sound is like a young pigeon
> > In the morning looking for me

Alcides described love with unashamed yearning. It was a relief to hear his eagerness. I worried that perhaps writing about Shakespeare's anti-ideal had reminded the students of their difficulties meshing two quite different cultures.

Notes for a Negative Love Poem

Step 1. To brainstorm for a series of negative comparisons, fold a large sheet of paper in half, making two long, narrow columns. At the top of one column write "Lover," and at the top of the other column write "Spring." As each element of the lover is listed, such as eyes, find something in spring that matches or enhances it. What in spring shines brightly or sparkles like a lover's eyes? Moon and stars, perhaps. Continue with comparisons for mouth, neck, hair, sound of voice, smell of breath, etc.

Step 2. To cut the sentimentality, make a list of negative comparisons. Eyes not like the sun, lips not red. When these comparisons are joined with the positive ones, they take on Shakespeare's cadence and sound like this:

> The sound of her voice isn't like the waterfall's, it is like the
> sound of a machine gun

or like this:

> My lover's eyes are brown like chocolate
> But not as sweet

Step 3. As in a recipe, assemble all the ingredients, using the form of one negative per line suggested by Shakespeare's poem. Recommend that students arrange their negatives from smaller to larger, ending with a proverbial bang.

The next day we returned to Rumi's poem. As soon as they heard that Rumi's poems spoke of love for Allah, the young ladies in the full hijabs perked up. They clearly felt more comfortable writing about spiritual than about carnal love. I was delighted that the poem fit their concept of what was comfortable and enjoyable. Months before, when we had read Tu Fu's poem, I had been afraid to broach the subject of travel. Suddenly, with Rumi's wonderful poem before us, with its references to camels and caravans, I hesitated no longer: "Write about home," I directed the class. "If you are looking for a way to respond to Rumi's poem, write about what you used to have and what you have now. Describe how you feel about what you have lost."

The students' poems and prose pieces about home were profound and true, some of the best things they had written all year. In these detailed evocations of home, the paradise which had slowly been gathering around them rose in full bloom. Shumi's ode to her Oromo village swayed in a meditative rhythm.

My Village

My village where I grew place
Where I played a free space
Where I made a lot of friends
O! my village, O! my friends
I miss you forever
I don't know... I don't know my home
When God says, I will see you one day

O! my home, my village
My grow place, free space
I feel empty in my heart
I need to hear the voice of horses, goats, cattle, and oxen
O! gorilla, do you remember that you woke us up?
Birds, do you remember that?
You pray early like human pastor sings
O! my flower, my lily
I miss Sukke [tree name], I miss Birribisa [tree name]
The big trees around my home
Why are you only there?
Why are you not here?
I pray to see you
I want to live with you forever
Speak with me Dhadhaba [river name] "duba dhuu dhudhaba"
Talk to me Anjelalo "duba dhuu anjelalo"
My long river you clean all the dirt away.

Shumi's intense longing not just for people, but for animals, trees, and the river which carried away dirt, throbbed with Rumi's inspiration: his direct address to lovers became her calls to friends, to gorilla, birds, lily, trees. His questions to the laggard travelers became her plaintive cries to those left behind: "Why are you only there? Why are you not here?" A sense of unreality pervaded Shumi's poem. Rumi was rousing the lovers to set off to a world yet being born; Shumi was experiencing the tearing realization that all she had loved was far away. Her own identity was challenged, as if she could not quite believe in herself far from her beloved village. "My grow place, free space" captured the essence of attachment: her entire life had suffused this place where she had been free of worry and grief and the awareness of being a stranger. Her poem had been unlocked by Rumi's experience of the divine and helped by Shakespeare's rich array of sense descriptions. In an instant, in a twinkling of an eye, as we say, Rumi's appeal beyond the stars had transported Shumi into the heart of her real home, where she could command to be remembered. This was the poem of a refugee, not an immigrant—a distinction I learned from the students. This was grief, gently but heart-stoppingly expressed. What the students created in Jane and Linda's extraordinary class was as much a part of their lives in flux as it was fixed on the page.

Since the success of this assignment startled me, I had to rely on second-guessing to fathom its appeal. From the start, I had planned to use poems from the students' own traditions. After all, to write with authority and passion, writers must believe that a sympathetic audience exists for their work somewhere in the world. Even the solitary poet Emily Dickinson sought engagement with "the world that never wrote to me." For students who have lost almost everything, especially those not schooled in their own literature, discovering their own literary tradition might very well call them forth on a creative journey. They might hear echoes of home which to their American teachers would remain mute. Also important, however, was the timing; it was clear that earlier in the year, the refugee students had little presence of mind to write about their lost homes and families. What Jane and Linda and I had developed—as much by hunch and experiment as reasoned rationale—looked in retrospect like this:

- Experiment with neutral description, playful comparisons, vocabulary building.
- Enjoy the communal reading and appreciation of each other's work.
- Tackle the demon of strangeness occasionally (wallowing in same could have been self-defeating).
- Allow students to converse with each other and the teachers about real things in their lives. (Jane and Linda became friends with some students in the class.)
- Return every so often to the subject of their pasts, especially through their own literary traditions.

It didn't hurt that we teachers took seriously the students' sturdy, curious, and steadfast intellects. We challenged them with readings that any native English speaker their age would have enjoyed and found rewarding. Jane and Linda grasped the students' predicaments and were deeply interested in their cultures. They disciplined when necessary, but they did not dismiss or demean their students. My sense was that we teachers felt honored to be working with the class. Maybe in the end, like Shumi, the students wrote as much for us as for each other and themselves.

At the end of the year, Jane and Linda published a large Xeroxed booklet of the students' writing. Excited to read to each other, the students planned a feast day of native foods. Maps and flags of their countries decorated the cover: Cambodia, Kurdistan, Ethiopia, Kenya, Argentina, Eritrea, Iraq. One young woman in full hijab handed around a plate of fried food: "Try it, try it," she urged. "It's hot." The bready mixture burned all the way down. None of the young women in hijabs would give me permission to quote their work. I assumed that they were nervous because they barely knew me. Though they wanted their work included in the class booklet, I, with my request to publish, was an unknown, and these young women were deeply conservative. Reading aloud in their own circle of classmates was part of the educational process, but publishing in the vast unknown of the United States—well, they had no idea what this meant and didn't want to risk (I assume) offending either religion or culture.

Having a reading had become the class's expected celebration of their writing. That day, with the full array of their year's work before them, no one chose to read embarrassing lunchroom stories, or songs of love and loss to their homelands. Instead, they presented essays about "what I want to be when I grow up" and zany interviews with fictional high-school characters. When I commented on this later, Jane and Linda chimed together, "They want to be happy and hopeful. They don't want to remember embarrassment."

Two years later, I learned that Shumi still had not passed the Minnesota Basic Standard Writing Test. Because she had not graduated from high school, she could not yet claim the scholarship that awaited her at a local technical college. With Linda's tutoring, she continued to try. Her husband, finally allowed to leave the Kenyan refugee camps, was compelled to settle in Norway. He had not been granted entrance to the United States.

NOTES

[1] I met Jane Sevald through my neighbor and fellow writer Linda Kantner. Jane's part-time ELL classes at Como Senior High School were her first teaching assignments in the St. Paul Public Schools. Before that, for twelve years she had taught adult literacy in the Minneapolis schools. Linda, with a master's in social work, has had numerous jobs in school systems. She has also published a number of vivid stories in regional and national magazines and anthologies, winning the *Minnesota Monthly* Tamarack Award for fiction in 2001 for her story "Night Noises."

[2] Shumi is Oromo, one of the largest language and cultural groups in East Africa. The Oromo were repressed by various regimes, especially by Ethiopia's Haile Selassie, whose policies divided them and taxed their largely agricultural economy at rates as high as 75 per-

cent. A revolt of Oromo peasantry in 1974 helped to oust Selassie, but the Oromo were not much better off under the following regime, which drafted them to fight against the Eritreans to the north. This war led to imprisonment and torture of many groups in Ethiopia, as did the civil war in Somalia during the 1990s. The Oromo and Somalis share about 30 percent of their respective languages. In the Twin Cities, they remain distinct populations but are not as full of enmity as are the Ethiopians and Oromo for each other. See Gadaa Melbaa, *Oromia: An Introduction to the History of the Oromo People* (Kirk House Publishers, 1988, 1999). Conversations with Jane Sevald and Linda Kantner enlarged my understanding of the Oromo culture. Note that Shumi's mother practiced the native Oromo religion as a child, converted to Islam as a teenager, and then to Christianity during her marriage.

[3]The Center for Victims of Torture is a valuable resource on post-traumatic stress syndrome and survivors of torture. Contact the Center at 717 E. River Rd., Minneapolis, MN 55455, www.cvt.org.

[4]Tu Fu, "Written on the Wall at Chang's Hermitage," *One Hundred Poems from the Chinese*, translated by Kenneth Rexroth (New Directions, 1971, p. 4).

[5]Mohamed Farid and Don McMahan, *Accommodating and Educating Somali Students in Minnesota Schools: A Handbook for Teachers and Administrators* (Hamline University Press, 2004). This master's thesis was published by Hamline University, where I teach in the Graduate School of Education and the Graduate School of Liberal Studies. When Barbara Swanson, my colleague and friend and, at the time, director of Hamline's Master's of Arts in education program, heard that I was venturing into ELL classrooms with students from East Africa, she gave me a copy of this small helpful book.

Helpful publications regarding the Hmong immigrants and the subsequent generation born in the U.S. include Mai Neng Moua, editor, *Bamboo among the Oaks: Contemporary Writing by Hmong Americans* (Minnesota Historical Society, 2002); and the literary magazine *Paj Naub Voice: A Journal Giving Expression to Hmong Voices* (published twice a year by the Hmong American Institute for Learning (HAIL), 2654 Logan Ave. N., Minneapolis, MN 55411).

[6]Stephen King, "The Body," *Different Seasons* (New American Library, Signet Edition, 1983). Though I saw the movie *Stand by Me*, based on "The Body," I liked the novella better. One of my favorite St. Paul teachers, Al Kvaal, used "The Body" with his remedial reading students at Harding High School, and together we taught his students to write a story based on elements from "The Body." Al gave out yearly awards for this assignment and allowed me to judge the stories for creativity. He named the awards "The Fortunato Awards" after me, which was almost more notoriety than I could bear, and which was a highlight of my early residency years.

[7]This quotation from Rumi on the Duluth Memorial to the victims of lynching is cited in www.claytonjacksonmcghie.org/disc_guide.pdf.

[8]Rumi, "Lovers," from *The Divani of Shams i Tabriz*.

[9]William Shakespeare, "Sonnet CXXX," *The Complete Works of Shakespeare*, edited by Hardin Craig (Scott Foresman and Co., 1961, p. 492).

CHAPTER THREE

Teaching in the Native American Spirit: South Dakota and Minnesota

I.

For a few years in the middle 1980s, I extended my circuit beyond Minnesota to North and South Dakota as a reciprocal agreement among the state arts boards invited writers to cross the borders. Driving west to South Dakota one October Sunday, I took Highway 12 through gently rolling farmland and small towns with their punctuation marks of water towers and grain elevators. It was a beautiful balmy day, the leafless trees giving off a gentle haze as I stopped in Litchfield for gas and a few jokes about the Minnesota Vikings football game on TV. Except for our conversation, the streets were intensely quiet; no one could have guessed that in 1862 during the six-week Dakota War, Litchfield had been the site of bloody battle between European settlers and the starving Dakota Indians. The war ended with an infamous hanging of thirty-eight Dakota, the number commuted by President Lincoln from over 300. Learning about the Dakotas' subsequent deportation to reservations in Nebraska had shocked me when I first moved to Minnesota. My familiar history texts had not breathed a word of this conflict, which came in the middle of the country's much greater civil conflict.[1]

Back on the road, I veered north to deserted Highway 28. No kids played ball in the still-green yards, but near the South Dakota border, a farmer was plowing his fields. Wallace Stevens' poem "Ploughing on Sunday" came to mind,[2] and I felt camaraderie with this lone figure guiding his ship under a wide arc of sky. We seemed linked by more than good weather. Turning up human soil for exposure to rain and sun was a poet teacher's work. When students dug into poetry, I never knew what they would unearth.

FARMERS REVIVAL—HEAR WHAT GOD SAYS ABOUT THE FARM CRISIS! A hand-lettered sign teetered crazily on the roadside. An arrow, rough as a scarecrow's claw, pointed down a dirt road. My mood darkened; farm women were protesting bank foreclosures, and farms that had been worked by the same families for generations were selling dirt cheap. In the Great Depression, my North Dakota grandfather bought up four farms for nothing more than back taxes. My mother had often bragged about his enterprising pluck, but she had never mentioned the families whom his purchases had displaced.

On the horizon, a mass of blue-gray clouds rose above the prairie. A green-and-white highway sign announced GLACIAL RIDGE TRAIL. I wondered fleetingly if the students I was about to meet would write about the farm crisis. Crossing a narrow bridge over the serpentine Little Minnesota River, I noted that its green water was sluggish compared to the muscular brown Minnesota River, which joined the Mississippi at Fort Snelling where the Twin Cities had begun. Just before the town of Browns Valley in Traverse County, a historical marker described an amateur archaeologist who had uncovered a broken skeleton in a gravel pit. The skeleton was estimated to have been buried about 6000 B.C. "The spot was then an island in the ancient River Warren, an outlet of glacial Lake Agassiz," I read, leaning from the car. Amused to be dished out knowledge as if I were ordering a hamburger from my car, I gathered that the skull had belonged to an adult male between twenty-five and forty years old with the physical characteristics of a North American Indian.[3]

Intrigued by this evidence of ancient civilization and the huge glacial lake whose gradual disappearance had deposited the rich soil of the Red River Valley, I thought again of the Dakota Conflict. Each side had suffered: pioneers whose rude homes had been burned, and the Dakota who had been forced off their hunting grounds and made wards of a government that ignored them. Looking over my shoulder, I spied far below a huge expanse of blue water: Lake Traverse, the origin of the Red River of the North. A Minnesota State Trooper waited in ambush just off the road. As I slowed, a white-and-black road sign announced CONTINENTAL DIVIDE 977 FEET. I was over the border. South Dakota welcomed me.

That evening, from my room at the Viking Motel, I phoned "Vicki," the contact teacher in the town I'll call Novelle, to discuss tomorrow's schedule. She startled me by saying, "I bet you're not prepared for Indian students." She was right about that. "There aren't so many in the high school as in junior high," she continued. "We have a hard time keeping them in school." Hearing the concern and resignation in her voice, I felt an odd disquiet. Was she telling me this to warn me that the students would be difficult? Or was she covertly hoping that my visit would engage the Dakota students and interest them in school? If that was so, I felt acutely unprepared. What I knew about Native Americans in Minnesota and the Dakotas could fit on a single line: Ojibwe in the northern forests, Dakota in the prairies. Thanking Vicki, I hung up, trying to squelch my anxiety with assurances that my circuit-writing experience would carry me through.

Vicki's twelfth-grade English class started before 8:00 the next morning. The small, second-floor classroom was crammed with desks. A model of William Shakespeare's Globe Theatre balanced on a storage cabinet, and banners and costume posters of Merrie Olde England brightened the walls. The Dakota students sat toward the back, long-legged and dark-haired. Blond, Nordic students filled the rest of the desks. No one glanced up as I entered. Seniors were hard to motivate, I knew; they already had one foot out the schoolhouse door. Plunging ahead, I wrote all five of my names, first, middle, family, and married, on the board: "Margot Rosalie Fortunato Kriel Galt." My husband, Fran Galt, had grown up in Mandaree, North Dakota. "His father was a missionary on the Mandan–Arikara–Hidatsa reservation," I told the class. Then I gulped: what would the Native American students think of being proselytized? Quickly I changed the subject: "My husband and I don't have kids in common. We have cats." Nobody laughed.

Desperation curdled in my stomach. I should stop trying to win them. I should flaunt my difference. "My Italian grandfather came to the U.S. in 1900, without a word of English," I announced. "He walked New York City all day, until at nightfall, he slumped on church steps unsure what to do. A policeman approached and questioned him." My voice brightened: "My grandfather answered in Italian. And guess what? The policeman spoke Italian. He took my grandfather home and gave him a spaghetti supper." Not a peep from the class. If I had stood on my head, these kids probably wouldn't have noticed. OK, I thought, let them close ranks against me. Then I realized maybe they were afraid to speak; maybe they were afraid of being ridiculed.

I changed tactics. "Please make a name tag," I said. Since I had told them my names, I would ask for theirs. "First names will be enough." I showed them how to fold notebook paper to stand up on their desks. As the names appeared, I walked around the room, reading them aloud: Bill, Kris, Lonnie, Jon. Then at the back I read, Big Red Running Brave. The minute the name came out of my mouth, the class snickered. This clearly was not the boy's name at all. He was pulling my leg. Yet, I didn't really mind. He had done me a favor: their laughter had loosened them up. There was also a subtle pride in his ruse; he had used an Indian stereotype to tease me, the stranger who maybe assumed the wrong things.

Even before entering the class, I had decided that we'd write grandparent poems. With younger students, the topic worked like a charm; affection skipped problematic parents and settled comfortably on grandparents. After Vicki's description of the Native American students, I wanted to make sure the first day's exercise crossed ethnic boundaries. In rural Midwestern life, no matter what your ethnic background, grandparents and elders are important.

> She got sick picking up apples
> on the hill behind the house. ...
> —John Calvin Rezmerski[4]

James Wright's "Two Postures beside a Fire" offered a similar tribute to a hardworking elder:

> ... my father, who broke stones
> Wrestled and mastered great machines ...[5]

We would write grandparent poems that acknowledged an admirable skill or quality in our elders. As I showed the class how to make a word web for brainstorming, it was hard to tell if they were listening. Finally, turning my back like a conductor on an audience, I began to draft my own poem on the board, about my Italian grandfather and the policeman who had befriended him. With other students, I might have read the first lines as I wrote them; I might have commented on how the poem would develop.

But with this bunch, I simply kept writing until I had reached a conclusion. Then I turned around. Most of the students were staring at blank sheets of paper. Squelching my disappointment, I reminded myself that older students often take longer to draft a poem than younger kids. Only in private would teenagers shuck their self-consciousness and write.

On Writing Grandparent Poems

Step 1. After telling a few stories about grandparents (teachers, tell yours too), have students close their eyes and imagine themselves doing something in a particular place with one of their grandparents. (Students without grandparents may choose to write about an older relative, a sister, uncle, mother, father.) The place may be in a kitchen baking cookies, a garage working on a mower, a basement playing with a train set, a garden planting tiny carrot seeds. Ask students to imagine looking for several details that make this place unique: a cat clock, rakes draped with rags, Grandpa's set of baseball caps.

Step 2. In the middle of a blank sheet of large white paper, have students write the name they call this grandparent. Surround the name with rays or roads to start a word map or word web. ("Word maps" or "word webs" are a brainstorming activity for almost any subject and can aid in drafting a poem or discussing a historical topic. The brief notes, arranged in a circle around a central theme, avoid a hierarchical selection and thus suggest links among all ideas that come to mind.) Off one of the roads, write where they imagined themselves and what they were doing: "in the kitchen, watching Papa Max give his canary a bath" or "in the red car driving to the store." Then, off other roads, write the details they imagined to set the place apart.

Step 3. Continuing around the word map, suggest topics for students to note: sounds and smells of the place, items of the grandparent's clothing and general physique and features, favorite grandparent sayings or gestures—favorite teases, questions, songs, etc. Add what the child and the elder have done together at other times. Keep these phrases brief. Add what the elder has taught the child: practical or more philosophical lessons. Sometimes these lessons are more intuited than spoken.

Step 4. To create a repeating refrain, have students circle a favorite phrase on their word maps. This phrase will become their poems' beginning lines as the students begin to draft their poems. Advise them to keep the lines short, and, yes, they should elaborate if new ideas come to them. Encourage them to use the repeating line occasionally and perhaps to end with it.

Note: Older students, high school and adult, will take this poem more into their own hands, casting it with more shades of interpretation than will usually occur in work by younger students. For a fuller discussion, see pp. 8–19 in my book *The Story in History: Writing Your Way into the American Experience* (Teachers & Writers Collaborative, 1992).

After Vicki's class, my other classes were with younger students, who were livelier and more responsive. But in these classes as well, Native American students kept their reserve. I was disheartened. After school, walking into town for cookies and prepackaged oatmeal, I felt as if I were being watched, not suspiciously but curiously, by a group of men in cowboy boots and long black hair tied with twists of hide. In small towns, any stranger is cause for scrutiny; adults eye the visiting circuit writer like fish circling bait. A line from a poem called "Main Street Strangers" by my South Dakota friend Margaret Hasse came to mind: "we feel stranger than we are."[6] That strangeness can be useful, allowing a circuit writer to catch revelations. But sometimes, we itinerants have to brave wide-open, embarrassing stares.

Closing the motel door behind me with a sigh of relief, I sank onto the bed and spread the students' poems around me. In the evening, as I often do, I kept to my room in the Viking Motel, and between blaring TVs next door and slamming truck doors outside, I hunched against the headboard, reading student poems in poor light. Sometimes I wondered if the truckers or tired commercial travelers had any idea how the dame in Number 7 dipped between magic and boredom. From the Novelle poems written that first day, I retain an image of an old man with a Nordic nickname who ate his lettuce with sugar and cream. Years before, my North Dakota grandfather Papa Max had done the same thing. And I, the Italian daughter of oil and vinegar, had been shocked. Do we remember only what we've seen before, or what sharply challenges our expectations?

Big Red Running Brave's joke and the other senior students' reticence had sapped my confidence for the next day. Yet, as all teachers must, I owed it to them to remain curious, and not let difficulties shut me down. The next morning, I asked Vicki to explain how the Dakota had come to live in what appeared to be a Nordic town. At the turn of the twentieth century, she told me, an allotment system had allowed Indian reservation land to be sold. Plots on many reservations had been bought by European Americans. In earlier pioneer days, a certain amount of intermarriage had also occurred between Native Americans and whites. This reminded me of the novelist Louise Erdrich, from the Turtle Mountain Ojibwe in North Dakota. She is part German, with a German last name.[7] Today, Vicki went on, Indians and whites do not mix much, and in school many Indian students drop out for jobs or marriage. "I don't expect to see Nina [a Dakota student] here much longer, though it's a shame." Vicki sighed. "Nina is a good student."

Recently, and more ominously, Vicki said, a Dakota girl had committed suicide in the bathroom at school. A tremor ran through me. Vicki's face was pale with concern, yet she did not elaborate. She was respecting the student's privacy, I thought. In education circles, teen suicide had only recently become a topic of discussion, as school counselors realized that students needed help grieving a friend's self-eradication. I remembered an incident from another school: the student who had found the suicide's body acted sick afterwards, often crying silent tears and putting her head down during class. When a teacher asked her what was the matter, a torrent of anguish had spilled out. The girl talked and talked, telling the story over and over again. When she had finally talked it out, she seemed to regain her equilibrium. Now, Vicki's information brought me alert, like a knife clanging against a tile floor. My lack of knowledge about the Dakota people seemed suddenly dangerous.

Feeling an extra urgency, I went to the school library, where I located pamphlets and self-published histories about eastern South Dakota, as well as several books about Native Americans in general, including Peter Matthiessen's *In the Spirit of Crazy Horse*,[8] and *Carriers of the Dream Wheel: Contemporary Native American Poetry*.[9] It was like learning how to swim in the middle of the ocean. In less than two weeks I had to inspire the students' trust and create exercises that would guide them into telling their own stories.

The poems in *Carriers of the Dream Wheel* were like nothing I had ever heard before:

> ... her smooth thighs pumping for a goal
> of ice-whiskey dresses and new dollar bills ...

> When I was a child ...
> ... I never saw a woman die
> from living.
> > —Anita Endrezze Probst[10]

> What's that—the noble savage?
> ... if he tries
> to teach you mountains
> or whisper imagined love
> to the tamarack ...
> > —James Welch[11]

> Gather your memories
> into a basket ...
> into your cornhusk bag.
> Your grandfather sings for us
> beyond the dry rustling cornstalks.
> > —Liz Sohappy Bahe[12]

In these poems, generations were linked together, struggling under a wide sky. The large scope made the confessional, I-centered poetry with which I was familiar seem self-involved and narrow by comparison. I felt sprung alert like the first time I had encountered the voices of Walt Whitman and Audre Lorde.

Searching for something I could use with Vicki's class, I happened on W. M. Ransom's "Statement on Our Higher Education for Ron Lampard, Nisqually," about the ethic of the hunt as well as a critique of what traditional western culture means by "higher education." Hunting seemed like a good topic; it might be a skill possessed by the Novelle students. After all, they lived on a prairie where game abounded. Though I was not interested in advocating hunting, I hoped to involve Dakota and Nordic students in writing about a subject common to both, and I wanted a Native American poet to be our guide.

For Native Americans, Ransom suggested, hunting was more than a

blood sport; it entailed an elaborate code of honor that included attentive-
ness and humility. Excited and anxious to hear how the students would re-
act, I read Ransom's poem to Vicki's class.

> We learned that you don't shoot
> things that are wiser than yourself:
> cranes, crippled bear, mountain beaver, toads.
> We learned that a hunter who doesn't eat his game
> is a traitor and should wander the earth,
> starving, forever.
> We learned to fish the shadow side of creeks
> and to check traps every morning before the dew lifts.
> It is a kindness in our savagery
> that we learned to owe our prey
> a clean death and an honorable end.
> We learned from our game
> to expect to be eaten when we die,
> learned that our fathers
> learned all this before us.
> Because of this you are brother
> to cranes, mountain beaver, toads and me.
> And to one old crippled bear
> that neither of us will ever see.
> —W. M. Ransom[13]

Silence greeted the conclusion, but it was a silence with resonance, the
silence of a forest where something has stirred.

The end of the poem raised a puzzling question: What had kept the
crippled old bear alive? When I asked this, hands rose around the room.
"Animals became canny after they are wounded," one student said as confidently and boldly as if he were instructing us on how to turn on a computer.
I did not need to feign naiveté. The fact is, I knew nothing about hunting
and fishing. "Why did the man fish in the shadows?" I asked, and, again,
hands rose around the room. "Fish hide in the shadows and are easier to
catch there than in the sun," a blond-haired student informed me. Vicki's
information of the early morning came back to me: in earlier years, white
settlers and Dakota natives had intermarried. Some blond students with
German or French or Scandinavian last names might very well be half or a
quarter Dakota. Furthermore, the students, whatever their ethnic back-

grounds, lived in the same environment and no doubt learned its lessons in similar ways. Perhaps I had been seeing the class's heritage too narrowly. It was time to acknowledge interconnectedness.

Ransom's poem and the discussion that ensued brought forth wonderful writing about hunting experiences. The students had absorbed some characteristics of poetry from the previous lesson; we brainstormed seasons, locales, hunting parties, prey, emotions, the closing in, and the kill. In one poem, a student described hunters spotting antelope, but since both humans and animals were tired, they all rested. When the hunt resumed, the antelope were standing:

> alert and beautiful with their white on
> their rumps, standing straight up. A
> shot rang through the coolies and an
> antelope fell after it took another good
> look at us and took three last steps
> of complete gracefulness.
> —Kevin A.

I was moved by the discipline with which Kevin honored the "three last steps" of the antelope; he could have chosen a much more dramatic but unwieldy detail. Also, his well-placed line breaks slowed the reader to almost breathless apprehension. His poem made clear that these hunters knew their prey in its animal grace and power.

In another poem, a girl constructed a more forthright morality tale:

> When we got to the other side, I could
> see through the willow shrubs the deer running
> hard and fast. My brother cursing at me for
> losing his tracks. But I didn't care. Just seeing
> him [the deer] fade away in the distance was good enough
> for me, the killing of our meanness.
> —Sheila I.

In both poems, students used local description to help us see the "coolies" (a local expression for *shallow valleys)*, and the willow shrubs where the deer ran fast. Like Ransom, Sheila had fractured a term (*savagery* in his case, *killing* in hers) into many ironic facets.

The ambiguity that guns could inspire turned from pride to sorrow in

"From Love to Steel," a beautiful poem written that day by Allen W., a junior. His poem, like so many other poems I've encountered about guns, was really a poem about a crucial relationship.

> Was I 9 or 10?
> My father stood proudly beside me.
> I had finally earned enough money
> To buy that big gun. I proudly stood
> Before my family with my hunting
> Attire and my new gun.
>
> My father and I enjoyed ourselves always
> When we hunted together. We were so
> Close, especially when we hunted. I
> Haven't touched the gun since he passed
> Away. Seems like there is no sparkle
> Or shine left in that gun. No feeling of closeness.
> Just hard, cold metal.

In other schools, when students had written poems about first guns, they usually symbolized a boy's passage into adulthood. Allen's poem began with this, but by the end of the poem, the gun had lost its romantic, ritualized appeal. Mourning the loss of his father, Allen also suggested that he had lost his place in the generation of hunters, who, as Ransom put it:

> learned that our fathers
> learned all this before us.

I hoped his classmates' poems would show him that the community of hunters extended across continents and encompassed Native Americans and settlers, ancient and modern.

Notes on Writing Hunting Poems

Step 1. Start with drawing a hunting scene, then labeling elements of landscape, plants, weather, and the prey. Remind students to put themselves in the drawings.

Step 2. Encourage students to linger on the different stages of the hunt, from sighting an animal to recognizing its characteristic gestures, vocalizations, movements. Encourage students to examine their feelings about hunting at various stages, from excitement to fear to numbness to elation to sorrow. Return to W. M. Ransom's ethical lessons learned in the hunt, and have students consider what they have learned.

Step 3. Describe using comparisons. Ask the simple questions of elements in the drawings: "What else does it look like?" Encourage students to suggest the mystery of stalking and killing and making use of another life. How does this mystery connect them to a cycle of existence larger than their individual lives?

After that second breakthrough day with Vicki's class, I decided to risk returning to "grandparent" poems, only with a new emphasis this time. The grandparent poems in *Carriers of the Dream Wheel* extended all generations—rebellious youth to wise elder—into wider connections. For many Native Americans, elders drew the cosmos together. They contained and passed on ancient wisdom; they conferred with the sun, moon, and stars; they transformed from their human form into mythological figures. As Anita Endrezze Probst wrote in "Red Rock Ceremonies":

> Owl Woman is blessing all directions. ...
> ... you are shaking purple in dusk,
> you are climbing the rims of the world.
>
> Old grandfather, we are combing your hair
> for blue stars and black moons. ...[14]

For the rest of the week, I read every day from the *Carriers of the Dream Wheel* anthology. Gradually, poems by Vicki's seniors and juniors trickled in. One Dakota student from Vicki's class wrote about the funeral of a relative who'd come back from Vietnam draped in the American flag. His relatives were very proud of that flag. "You know, Navajos made an unbreakable code during World War II!" the student told me.

Toward the end of the second week, another student in Vicki's class wrote an unusually perceptive poem about Native American longing for the old ones and the old ways:

> The grass is beginning to grow.
> Earth lets the new life spring forth from
>   her womb.

All creatures show their joy to see
   the beauty all around.
I see all of this as I walk in my search
   for what we have lost.
I seek to stop the weeping.
The People cry in their loneliness and
   their longing for the Old Ones and
   the Old Ways.
But what they cry for has been gone
   for too long and
Only the Oldest of the Grandmothers remember.
Finally my footsteps stop and slowly turn
   heading back to the New.
The People will continue to weep for
   that which has been lost can't return.
The Old Ways are gone leaving us only
   with a memory and emptiness and
   yearning.
But we will continue as we have always
   continued.
                              —Chris R.

This deeply moving poem of memory, loss, and yearning taught me more about contemporary Indian life than anything else Vicki's students had written. Other students, from, I assumed, German or Scandinavian backgrounds, wrote sympathetic portraits of individual grandparents or of parents exhausted by work, but they did not portray their elders as a force linked to ancient but diminishing power. Chris implied that none of her people desired change. Instead, they wept for the dim outline of their former ways.

Former ways, Nordic style, were showcased in town over the weekend at a holiday bazaar hosted by a church women's guild. The folk arts of weaving and *rosemaling* (Norwegian flower painting on wood) made bright backgrounds for conversation over teacups and plates of little sandwiches, reminding me of the cream-cheese blue moons and green stars that my sister and I used to make for my mother's tea parties. Crowded in among the wares, I found myself telling a few of the genteel, nicely dressed women about teaching at the public school. Curious to hear what they would say about the local Dakota people, I expressed my growing appreciation for the Native American students. Perhaps I "lay it on too thick," as my mother would have admonished. A few of the women responded with guarded criticism of "Indian drunks and Indian TB and Indian welfare families." Listening, I felt the same tremor of resistance and fear that racism in my southern childhood used to evoke.

The following week another Dakota girl attempted suicide in school. Shaken, I breathed a huge sigh of relief when she survived. But what would she do, I wondered, when she woke up to the aftermath of her despair? Knots of students talked about the suicide in the halls. She had been a middle-school student, not one whom I had taught. More attuned to the students than before, I sensed their desire to be gentle with one another. Now that I had encountered prejudice in the town, I appreciated more fully that the students did not seem to shun each other, though their different groups did not hang out together. Perhaps the suicide attempt had been a copy of the first, one of those disturbing mimicries that sometimes plague a school. Since Vicki did not address the suicide during any of my classes, I did not feel free to ask students to write about it. But I wondered what they might have said. Perhaps, like me, they would have recognized it as a cry for help. I sensed that they would have responded with empathy.

By the end of my two weeks, Vicki's seniors had thawed. Energy flowed in their discussion and writing. Maybe poetry had revitalized a circuit already in place, or maybe it had created new links. Later, when the town newspaper printed a whole sheet of student poems, I was very gratified. I knew that Vicki had contacted the paper at the beginning of the residency; she had wanted to make the community aware of the students' writing. Like other small-town newspapers, this one noted townspeople's comings and goings, marriages and funerals, buyings and sellings. In the published student writing, several fine poems about Dakota life were included, notably Chris's. I wondered what the town ladies would think when they read it. They would have a hard time dismissing it, I thought. There were plenty of poems about other topics: the pleasures of music and sports, memories of summer and farm life:

> He works hard in the field trying
> (hard) to get his crop out, trying

to keep his family out of a rut.
—Andree H.

... there he is
Dirty and tired in a 40-
Thousand dollar tractor
He'll never pay for.
—Ron O.

Clearly the farm crisis existed in the area, but it did not seem to have devastated these families. Or were the students employing proverbial Nordic—and Dakota—understatement? By this time, I had begun to see the students as individuals, beyond race and ethnicity; their stark, wise, honest voices rang with the bleached beauty and unrelenting wind of their high prairie. Now, it was time for me to depart. I am always leaving town just as hunches are turning into certainties and revelations growing leaves. I couldn't stay around to see whether attitudes evinced at the church bazaar would prevail or whether other patterns might flourish.

Later, my friend and fellow writer Margaret Hasse put some geographical and temporal perspective around my Novelle residency. As a native of Vermillion, South Dakota, on the Nebraska border, she helped me see South Dakota as divided into "east river and west river." East of the Missouri River, "you stood more than a fighting chance at having a successful farm," she told me. "But west of the river in the 'land of the burnt thigh,' is some of the poorest land in the United States, and seven Indian reservations." There on the Pine Ridge Indian Reservation had occurred the 1975 shoot-out between the FBI and members of the American Indian Movement (AIM), described in Peter Matthiessen's *In the Spirit of Crazy Horse.* AIM had stepped in to protect the Oglala Sioux from the murderous racism of whites and the abusive power of their own tribal leaders. Far bloodier and more protracted than any altercation Margaret had seen in Vermillion, the Pine Ridge conflict underscored the Indians' unfortunate legacy of alcoholism, poverty, and powerlessness. AIM had been founded in an effort to counteract that legacy and to build Native stability and the recognition of treaty rights. As part of this effort, AIM had also inspired Indian survival schools where Native languages and tribal culture were taught and celebrated.

Margaret showed me copies of a magazine called *Time of the Indian,* which had gathered Indian students' writing from survival schools in the Twin Cities and around Duluth. Before the mid-twentieth century, Indian education had usually followed a boarding-school model that often distanced Native American children from their language and culture. In the 1970s, Margaret had been a visiting poet at an Indian boarding school at Chamberlain, South Dakota. When she distributed copies of *Time of the Indian*, the boys and girls at Chamberlain had "crowded together to read the magazines." Even though she used example poems in the classroom from Native American anthologies and books and got a good response, she had found the poetry residency at Chamberlain a troubling experience. "Although teachers and counselors appeared to genuinely care for the students, still, the Indian youth were gathered from far distances, living in dormitories. Although there were Indian-based cultural activities, the legacy of Carlisle [Indian School] and other culture-killing Indian boarding schools is a dark legacy to overcome." Margaret commented that she wished a Native American poet had been sent to Chamberlain because "there was a hunger for role models about Indian culture." My experience of teaching across the cultural divide certainly bore this out. When Native American writers were not available, using Native writing as models became even more important.

The *Time of the Indian* programs, sponsored by COMPAS, the St. Paul-based poets-in-the-schools program, had continued for over a decade, during the 1970s and 1980s, part of the national multicultural revival spawned by the civil rights movement.[15] Had I known about this program and been bolstered with copies of *Time of the Indian*, I might have approached teaching Dakota students more confidently. As it was, the shock and insecurity of my initiation had burned it into my psyche.

II.

Esther Nahgahnub's dream catchers spun slowly in the dappled light of her backyard arbor. The huge platter-sized webs were first made to gather and dissolve her foster children's "night terrors"; now she said she made them for victims of AIDS. My collaboration with Esther began about ten years after Novelle; I was eager to continue learning about Native Americans and whites, this time among adults.[16] Esther, of the Fond du Lac band of the

Lake Superior Ojibwe, had agreed to a video project. Yet videographer Beni Matias, from Puerto Rico via New York, and I had approached the undertaking with trepidation. Would we be welcome on reservation land?

Esther removed the body from a flicker, then spread its wings to reveal the bird's golden under-feathers. Her dream catchers were composed mostly of roadkill. The flicker, which she had wrapped in newspaper, was one I'd found near my house and salvaged from being run over again and again. In her hands, taxidermy was a spiritual exercise. "Working with these feathers and hide teaches me that death is part of a circle." Unfortunately, the Minnesota Department of Natural Resources was not apt to agree. She had to fight diligently to win a variance from the department to use migratory bird feathers in her dream catchers, arguing that old treaties gave Native people the right to use roadkill plumage or hide. "My people have always known death," she explained in the video. "Whether from roadkill or winter kill or kills for food." Thinking about this later, I realized that mainstream Americans such as myself tended to resist the entirety of the cycle; we loved talking about "recycling," but not when the cycle referred to life-and-death. The days when family women prepared a dead relative for burial are long past. Many Americans live urban-style, where kills for food are so sanitized, shrink-wrapped, and frozen that we forget the winged and hoofed creatures who once carried the meat on their backs.

No wonder teachers taking their master's degrees, to whom I later showed Esther's video, were sometimes unsettled or offended. Elementary teachers especially: "We don't want to teach our students about death," some said. A perplexing refusal, considering that we do teach children about "health" and "illness," and deaths occur even in the most saccharine tales of childhood (consider *Bambi*). But mainstream education keeps everything within the sanitizing margins of a discipline. You can dissect flies in biology class, but you can't touch the carcass of a bird in art class. "We certainly wouldn't want to encourage our students to pick up dead animals and birds." Perhaps with fears of avian flu spreading worldwide, this was not a bad prohibition, but I suspected that the elementary school teachers were veiling their own distaste with concerns for their students. I led them in a careful discussion in which we considered death as part of a circle, acknowledging that healing art often referred to emblems of the departed, that many of the world's religions spoke frankly about death, and that we could make meaningful art from animals killed on the road. Interestingly, in contrast to their teachers, elementary students who saw Esther's video had no trouble at all with her using roadkill. Dream-catcher books were, by then, common in elementary classrooms; many students made their own dream catchers, which they hung from schoolroom ceilings, tiny bits of Native American protection and comfort, turning in the heating drafts.

Compromise is the nature of the circuit-writing life. I managed to convince the teachers to let the students see the video by proposing that we respond with a rather abstract exploration of the life cycle. I would ask the students to draw circles and write circle poems in the spirit of the dream catcher. To assist them, I suggested they structure their poems as a list of natural elements that they might put on a dream catcher, and then associate themselves with each tiny bit of fur, feather, or moss. "Fur for the gentleness of the rabbit," as Esther said, or "owl feathers for the vigilance of the owl." Equating traits valued in human life with elements in nature made perfect sense to children used to reading about raccoons in pinafores and trees that talk. By gently insinuating human life into a circle drawn through all living things, the exercise suggested that animals, trees, stars, and rivers indeed had vigorous, valiant lives, worthy of human emulation and protection.

The Gist of Circle Poems

Students draw circles inspired by the circle of life. Around the circles they write specific things from the natural world, prompted by categories. For example, if a teacher says "tree," students might write "Maple." Other categories might include some kind of water (ice, waterfall, river, etc.), a flower, a food plant, a mammal, something in the sky (clouds, moon, Mercury, etc.), a kind of weather or a season, a form of landscape (plateau, beach, island, etc.), a reptile, bird, and so on. Once there are eight or ten items around the circle, students connect two for their first line of poetry. This poem is inspired by well-known Kiowa writer N. Scott Momaday's "The Delight Song of Tsoai-Talee."

> I am a feather on the bright sky
> I am the blue horse that runs in the plain ...[17]

A child's first line might read something like "I am the raccoon in the green rain." As other elements from the circle are connected, the teacher might suggest, "Use a color in this line," or "Use an emotion or state of being in this line." See the full exercise in *The Story in History*, pp. 125–130.

The video footage, which Esther asked be shot by her son, though less professional than that of a practiced videographer, captured Esther's slow and patient pace on long summer afternoons as she rambled the woods, looking for lichen, raven feathers, bits of fur. What it did not capture was the difficulty Esther, Beni, and I—three women from quite different backgrounds—had communicating both simple things like setting times to meet and more complicated things like determining what kind of equipment Esther's son needed to videotape her work. There was also confusion and hard feelings about payment for our project. Each of us had received a stipend from the supporting grant but, as with most arts funding, it scarcely compensated us at a decent rate. In the video's final editing the tension among us was smoothed away, but I sensed that we viewed each other across a divide carved by history's ugly scars: white appropriation of Native land, failed treaty obligations, and subsequent Native loss and mistrust. Though the video was a tribute to our desire to work together, I was not sure we would speak again.

A few years later, I commissioned a dream catcher from Esther. She used flicker feathers like the ones I had brought her while we worked on the video. The feathers seemed to me a good omen. The big web with its yellow feathers hung in my writing room, and the video, which I continued to show to all kinds of students, drew tears from adults who had fought in the Iraq war. Esther's big webs with their feathers and hide circled us gently into the dream catchers' sacred message of sorrow and healing and reminded me again of Esther's generosity of spirit.

III.

In her novel *Power*, Native American poet and novelist Linda Hogan describes a single look exchanged between two elders of the vanishing Florida Taiga Indians. The narrator, a teenage girl, is watching the elders in a courtroom, where one of them is being tried for shooting an endangered Florida panther.

> ... there is something between them. Their eyes speak and I can't enter the current of their gaze. It's an exchange the color of rich, muddy water. I know a world grows there, in that water, the river flowing between them. Maybe it is a river of life or the deep water of our tribe and in it are our riches.[18]

The same year that *Power* appeared in print, I happened to be teaching at a public school on the White Earth Ojibwe reservation in northwestern Minnesota. It was there that I had the chance to understand Hogan's book in a new light, to consider the third pair of eyes in that exchange in the courtroom, the attentive, silent stare of the teenage girl.

Passing me in the hall, a White Earth Ojibwe student lifted her chin and pursed her lips slightly. "We recognize each other in this protective silence," said her look. I had been introduced to her through a relative who worked at the school, the only Ojibwe so employed. I drove out to the reservation and visited the family; they greeted me warmly, and talked about White Earth history, which was similar to that in Novelle, with Native land being purchased by whites in the early twentieth century. Observing the Ojibwe extended family, with aunts interacting with nieces much as Euro-American parents tease, admonish, and guide their children, I felt gently educated to the persistence of traditional ways. When I said good-bye, the teenage girl told me, "I will greet you tomorrow with this look," and she raised her chin slightly and pursed her lips. "It is our silent greeting we keep among ourselves and our friends. We know we can trust each other." This brought me inside a private circle, one not shared with everyone, and I left, wondering if Native people had developed this as a silent greeting in the forest, centuries ago, or if Indian children had exchanged such a look as token of solidarity in white-run boarding schools.

In the 1920s, Fern Krauschner attended a Native American boarding school in Pipestone, Minnesota.[19] Located all the way across the state from her home on the Mississippi River, Pipestone Indian School drew students from all directions. When Fern entered at age six, she spoke no English; the military style of organization, the uniforms of green slacks and dresses, and the harsh dormitory life disoriented her. "The U.S. government policy had been to take Indian children away from their culture," she told me, "make them forget how to speak their language, [give up] Indian dancing." When she first entered school, she didn't even know her Christian name because, as she said, "My family called me Wenona, the Dakota name for firstborn girl."

Fern's isolation stemmed from her people's suspicion of whites, who had imprisoned and sent them to a reservation in Nebraska after the 1862 Dakota War. They had escaped the Nebraska reservation, "traveling by night and hiding by day." Eventually they had settled on large Prairie Island in the Mississippi River. Not recognized by the government for sixty years, the Prairie Island Dakota survived by fishing, hunting, planting gardens, and raising barns and houses. Sitting by the bed of this stalwart woman, ill with Lou Gehrig's disease, I found myself swimming in a different concept of time. Fern spoke familiarly of ancestors centuries before; her great-grandparents had been children of Chiefs Wabasha and Red Wing. Her people had once lived in Michigan; they had seen "blond men with horns," possibly the Vikings. In 1851, whites had burned her people's village in Red Wing. Yet on Prairie Island, Fern had known many whites who spoke and read her Dakota language. The rather guttural Dakota language, with its stately cadence, dropped in pitch at the end of a sentence or question. This and its slow pace gave it quite a different effect from English. Dakota also carried evidence of the Dakota Conflict in the speech of children raised by the grandmothers and mothers who had survived: the children used almost entirely feminine endings. Yvonne Kelly,[20] a Mississippi Choctaw by birth but a student of Dakota language and culture, explained that since the Dakota consider their language to be feminine, men must put a male ending on statements, prayers, sayings, and stories. To say "Peace" in Dakota creates a phrase—*Chautewashteyon nap-chiyuzapee yay*—meaning filled with joy or elation. To honor someone in greeting would be to say "We honor you with peace, with a good heart." The *yay* at the end is feminine, identifying the conclusion of the sentence and the speaker's gender. A male would end with *yay doe*.

After finishing with Fern's interview I presented it to Kari Dietrich's sixth-grade students at Red Wing's Twin Bluff Middle School.[21] A few Prairie Island Dakota were in these classes. Fern had been eager that students of all kinds hear her story. Approaching oral history and Native concepts of time, I began by having students write personal Winter Counts, based on the Dakota oral calendar. (See *The Story in History*, pp. 108–117, for a fuller discussion of Winter Counts.) Some of the Winter Counts I had read or seen reached back into the 1700s. For the oral culture of the Dakota people, the Winter Count represented not a census or a survey but a mnemonic or illustrated device for counting and recalling each year. Some tribes created a short rhythmic phrase for each year; others added to this a small drawing as part of a larger Winter Count hide or cloth which contained a picture for each year. Every winter a Dakota band would select an event to represent that year. Then the person in charge of keeping the Winter Count would commit it to memory, and in some bands add a drawing to the accumulated images for past years. As I understood the practice, bands would then "count" their history at their leisure (and they had more leisure in the winter); each short line and small picture stood for a much longer story. Since some Winter Counts, eventually written down in the 1920s, contained hundreds of entries, it is understandable that the lines would be short, to aid in memorization. For example,

   1789 [English translation] Crows/ many/ they freeze to death

   1801 They break out/ with a rash.[22]

These compressed, telegraphic lines (in modern parlance, a cross between a headline and a haiku poem) provided excellent guidance for students to write vividly about their own much shorter life spans. As the Red Wing sixth-graders were all around twelve or thirteen years old, and had shared many life experiences, it was fun to take a line from each student's personal Winter Count and make a comprehensive, classroom Winter Count.

   1989 Threw up green Jell-O on Dad, Spring (Joe)

   1992 Called 911, couldn't put on socks, Summer (Amanda)

   1996 My sister's cat Patches knocked down Christmas Tree, Winter (Ryan)

   1999 Fractured index finger at Nybo's, Summer (Nate)

The Gist of Writing a Personal Winter Count

Step 1. Start with making a word map of vivid memories in a student's life. Emphasize that these do not need to be in chronological order: memory bounces around from moment to moment, season to season. Give students cues to spark ideas, such as "Write a memory of a holiday, birthday, etc., or an accident, or an embarrassing moment, or sibling rivalry, or a fun surprise, or a silly kiddish thing you did. Write about an animal or a pet, about a death in the family or the nation, about an unusual public event that marked a season for you. Write about a favorite toy or game." Encourage conversation among students to spark memories. Students should not expect to remember back earlier than three or four years old. Family photos or stories will help them collect bits of information about themselves as babies. Have students write these tidbits on their word maps.

Step 2. Now write the actual years of their lives—1990, 1991, 1992, etc.—down the long side of a piece of unlined white paper. A child born in 1990 would begin with that year and proceed to 2005. With older students or adults, have them write only their first ten or fifteen years. The lines that accompany each year should be compressed, with vivid details, and perhaps a few items connected together. Remind students that each line stands for a much longer story. End each line with the season when it reasonably happened. If students can't remember precisely the age they did something, have them make a reasonable guess at their age. Remember that we don't turn one year old until the second year of our lives.

Drawing upon the success of the personal Winter Counts, I asked the sixth-grade classes to write a Town Winter Count for Red Wing. Each student was given two Xeroxed pages from a town history book from which to derive his/her entry:

> 1853 Dr. Sweeney confronted with his first communicable disease problem—Asiatic cholera (Kyle)
>
> July 21, 1861 First Minnesota Regiment saw action early in the Civil War, took part in bloody Battle of Bull Run (author unknown)
>
> 1868 Early stock company played in Music Hall; earlier public lectures, concert, German theater, and Black minstrels (Alyssa)
>
> July 13, 1890 Red Wing's greatest tragedy, boat named *The Sea Wing* capsized in tornado winds on Lake Pepin; steamer arrived in Red Wing with 42 bodies on board; 23 more found, some alive. Hats, chairs, and other stuff recovered from lake (Maria) [Note:

Lake Pepin is an expansive, lake-sized part of the Mississippi River, just south of Red Wing]

1905 Red Wing Shoe Company incorporated on Feb. 10th (Cole)

1913 Speed limits established (Dustin)

Though we were using a Native American form, I noticed that the town history contained little about the Dakota people. When, for instance, did the burning of Chief Red Wing's village occur? When did the Dakota Conflict take place? When did this systematic amnesia set in?

To offset this absence, I handed out some excerpts from my interview with Fern and asked the students to create a Winter Count based on her life. As with their own personal Winter Counts, the one for Fern had intimacy and vivacity of feeling and detail, whereas the town Winter Counts and the Dakota Winter Counts focused on experiences that an entire community had witnessed, suffered, and recalled. Fern's difficulties at Pipestone Indian School, particularly the matrons' whipping children with a razor strop and making them kneel on the cold floor for hours on end, stunned the kids. With no corporal punishment in their school, the contemporary Red Wing students could not conceive of a child as young as Fern had been—six or seven—being naughty enough to deserve such harsh punishment. They worried about her: wasn't she cold and hungry as she knelt on the floor? Did her sister or friends sneak her food? Wouldn't whipping with a razor strop break the skin and make her bleed? Who took care of her wounds? When I handed each student several sheets from Fern's interview, they eagerly scanned the typed text. They wanted to know what she had said on other sheets. The next day their curiosity was rewarded when I read to them the class's "Winter Count for Fern," dateless because Fern, like many other Native Americans, measured time in relation to family events—births, deaths, marriages, moves, harsh winters, etc.—the same sense of time reflected in the Dakota Winter Counts.

Stayed in dormitory at Pipestone Indian school. Now dream of going back there, cry in my sleep because I dreamed of going back to Indian School. (Ashley)

The school was like military, with uniforms and bells when done with chores. (Jake)

At school, kids strapped with old-fashioned razor-sharpening strops; got Buster Brown haircuts. (Sara)

Had to line up from smallest to biggest; only eight people to a table. (Robert)

Stuck up for sister, got punished. (Nick)

Girl moved during haircut, got stabbed with scissors. (Edward)

Some entries the students wrote about Fern's history were not entirely coherent. Oral history interviews require sophisticated historical knowledge to interpret, especially Fern's, which had a large, fluid scope. The classes had discussed the Dakota Conflict and Fern's account of her people meeting blond-haired strangers in early days, but it would have taken a much more thorough history lesson to make Fern's comments entirely clear to the class. Yet, Fern's history moved many students to write quick "Little Poems for Fern Krauschner." Her illness with its creeping debility shocked them; they knew she was paralyzed in arms and legs, and soon would be unable to breathe. Yet her courage and stamina, living years beyond doctors' predictions, made her vivid to them.

Many of the students' "Little Poems for Fern Krauschner" used repeating lines, a device they had perfected in other exercises. The "Little Poems" distilled the best of her interview. My favorites described Pipestone Indian School and her happy summers on Prairie Island after spending nine months away. She and her siblings and cousins fished in Buffalo Slough, danced around the table with Grandpa and Grandma, and reclaimed, as Hannah M. wrote, "The feel of being young":

> Oh the feel of being young
> The feel of powder between my fingers
> The feel of fry bread on my tongue
> The feel of Grandma's warm house
> The feel of Grandma's good food
>
> Oh the feel of grass between my feet,
> The feel of the warm flowing stream
> The feel of dancing again
> The feel of the beating drums
>
> The feel of being young.

Several months had passed since the interview. We were not sure that Fern would still be alive. Within a week came a note from her daughter, thanking the students for their work and saying that Fern had been very glad that they understood her history. Teaching in the Native American spirit, my first concern is for Indian students, but also for non-Indians. Indian ghosts lift from trees, step from fields of corn. It is a question of learning, as Esther Nahgahnub said, "to listen, to feel, to honor all things."

2000 Fern Krauschner passed away.

NOTES

[1]For information about the Dakota War or Dakota Conflict, as it is often called, see *Through Dakota Eyes: Narrative Accounts of the Minnesota Indian War of 1862*, edited by Gary Clayton Anderson and Alan R. Woolworth (Minnesota Historical Society Press, 1988). This book collects firsthand accounts from many sources and is vital for understanding the war from many points of view.

[2]Wallace Stevens, "Ploughing on Sunday," *The Collected Poems of Wallace Stevens* (Alfred A. Knopf, 1967). When I was casting about for a Ph.D. thesis topic in American Studies, I spent several years reading Stevens' work. Though I went on to write a novel about civil rights and Gullah oystermen from coastal South Carolina for my thesis, Stevens' poetry remained with me as a lyric, speculative voice, laying its imagery across my life.

[3]For more information on Browns Valley Man, see June Drenning Holmquist, Sue E. Holbert, and Dorothy Drescher Perry, *History Along the Highways: An Official Guide to Minnesota State Markers and Monuments* (Minnesota Historical Society, 1967); and Dorothy Perry Kidder and Cynthia A. Matson, *A Supplement to History Along the Highways: 1967–1972* (Minnesota Historical Society, 1973).

[4]John Calvin Rezmerski, "Grandmother," *25 Minnesota Poets #2* (Nodin Press, 1977, pp. 60–61). One of my favorite poems from the *25 Minnesota Poets* anthologies, I taught "Grandmother" again and again, and included it in *The Story in History* (Teachers & Writers Collaborative, 1992, pp. 14–16).

[5]James Wright, "Two Postures beside a Fire," *Collected Poems* (Wesleyan University Press, 1951, 1971, p. 161). Wright's poignant poem to his father describes a visit in which the old man sleeps while the son, bringing nothing home except himself, witnesses the restless twitching of his own hands.

[6]Margaret Hasse, "Main Street Strangers," *Stars Above, Stars Below* (New Rivers Press, 1984, p. 51). Margaret's second poetry collection, *In a Sheep's Eye, Darling* (Milkweed Editions, 1988), also became a favorite in my teaching kit. My interview with Margaret about South Dakota took place in spring 2005, in St. Paul. For a number of years we shared a poetry group in common, and I worked with Margaret when she was director of COMPAS

Writers in the Schools. Later executive director of Minnesota Alliance for Arts in Education and regional chair of the Kennedy Center Alliance for Arts Education, she currently serves as a consultant to state and national nonprofit arts and education organizations.

[7]Louise Erdrich's first few novels about her region and people, especially *Love Medicine* (Harper & Row, 1984) and *Tracks* (Henry Holt, 1988), are unmatched, it seems to me, in capturing the fluid and surreal blend of histories and cultures that make up the far northern border land between Minnesota and North Dakota, which is her territory. Erdrich's mother was French Ojibwe and her father German American. Erdrich was born in Little Falls, Minnesota, and grew up in Wahpeton, North Dakota, where her parents taught in Bureau of Indian Affairs schools. She is a member of the Turtle Mountain Band of the Ojibwe.

[8]Peter Matthiessen, *In the Spirit of Crazy Horse* (Viking Adult, 1980, 1983).

[9]*Carriers of the Dream Wheel: Contemporary Native American Poetry*, edited by Duane Niatum (Harper & Row, 1975). Though many other collections of Native American poetry have appeared since this one, it remains a favorite teaching book with its appealing design and a photo and biography accompanying each poet's selection.

[10]Anita Endrezze Probst, "The Truth about My Sister and Me," *Carriers of the Dream Wheel*, pp. 166–167.

[11]James Welch, "Directions to the Nomad," *Carriers of the Dream Wheel*, p. 253.

[12]Liz Sohappy Bahe, "Once Again," *Carriers of the Dream Wheel*, pp. 12–13.

[13]W. M. Ransom, "Statement on Our Higher Education for Ron Lampard, Nisqually," *Carriers of the Dream Wheel*, p. 198.

[14]Probst, "Red Rock Ceremonies," *Carriers of the Dream Wheel*, pp. 164–165.

[15]*Angwamas Minosewag Anishyinabeg: Time of the Indian*, edited by James L. White (COMPAS, 1975). The student writers published here were Ojibwe or Anishinabe. The Indian students I encountered in South Dakota were, I assume, part of the larger Dakota nation.

[16]Esther Nahgahnub is not only an artist and writer. She is also an activist for her people and the earth. In July 2000, she and Frank Koehen organized and led a Native American Spirit Journey around Lake Superior, to draw attention to destruction of the Great Lakes and damage to the world's fresh water supply. See www.nativecalling.org/archives/list2000.html.

My oral history project with Ojibwe artist George Morrison had encouraged me to work with Esther. George had grown up on the shores of Lake Superior near the town of Grand Marais, and his art in its later guises drew on Native American traditions and the lake landscape. The book we wrote together about his life and art, which I called an oral history memoir, was published in 1998 by the Minnesota Historical Society as *Turning the Feather Around: My Life in Art*.

[17]N. Scott Momaday, "The Delight Song of Tsoai-Talee," *Carriers of the Dream Wheel*, p. 89.

[18]Linda Hogan, *Power* (W. W. Norton, 1998, p. 139). My book group, composed of writers, read this novel in the fall of 2004. At the same time, *Audubon* magazine featured a story on "Playing Politics with the Florida Panther" (September-October 2004). Because

Minnesota has had success stories reintroducing timber wolves and protecting the bald eagle, our group didn't want to imagine a North American species rendered extinct in our lifetimes. Now when I think back on our reading of Hogan's story, I see a connection between the Florida panther, threatened by human intrusion into its habitat, and her teenage heroine, a Native American girl who wavers in her choice of identity between the dwindling tribe and an assimilated white identity.

[19]I conducted the interview with Fern Krauschner through the auspices of the Goodhue County Historical Society in Red Wing, Minnesota. As with most communities, one needs an introduction to the Prairie Island Dakota near Red Wing. Char Henn, director of the Historical Society, accompanied me for two visits to Fern's home on Prairie Island. I am many times indebted to the Historical Society for their support of my oral history projects in Red Wing. Transcripts of the interviews are housed in the library at the Historical Society. I also owe a very pleasant debt of appreciation to the Anderson Center for Interdisciplinary Studies outside Red Wing, where Robert Hedin, director, publisher, and poet, has welcomed me and many other scholars, writers, and artists for fruitful residencies and enlightening public programs.

[20]Yvonne Kelly was a student of mine in a class called "Journal and Memoir Writing" offered through the College of Continuing Education at the University of Minnesota. For the assignment to write a personal Winter Count, she turned in two: one in English and one in Dakota. This led to an interesting exchange between us about the language and its development. As she helped me craft a Dakota rendition of the greeting "We honor you with peace, with a good heart," she used phonetic spelling, not the orthography developed to render oral Dakota.

[21]I have had a number of invigorating residencies with Kari Dietrich and her sixth-grade classes, plus a fun-filled journal-writing in-service for the entire Twin Bluff staff. My earlier residencies with Kari's classes involved writing about Red Wing history and included the various exercises described here. The Winter Counts and poems for Fern Krauschner went into a readers theater script that I created from Red Wing oral histories and student writing.

Kari and her husband Dan Dietrich have contributed significantly to gathering and interpreting eastern Minnesota history. I count both of them among my friends.

[22]This excerpt comes from a much longer segment of Ben Kindle's Winter Count, first begun by the Oglala Sioux in 1759, and recorded in 1924. See *The Story in History*, pp. 111–113, for a longer excerpt and discussion of Winter Counts.

Chapter Four

Adams Spanish Immersion:
Writing and Hispanic Culture

I.

Below the Mississippi River bluffs, Adams Spanish Immersion nestles among floodplain cottonwoods and the bungalows of its St. Paul neighborhood. On winter mornings, it was a precarious slide from my house on the bluffs down to Adams' bright-faced, brick building. Once a traditional neighborhood school with white walls and desks in strict rows, Adams now sports Spanish phrases—*Bienvenido*—and a rainforest mural in its atrium. It also has acquired a statue of a *Peanuts* figure from the comic created by St. Paul native Charles Schulz. Lucy's skirts had been decorated by Señor Arredondo's morning kindergarten class. From the moment I met Heidi Bernal, Adams contact teacher and a native Minnesotan, I knew that my work at Adams would be lively and multicultural. Heidi's two boys romped with the dark sparkle of their Mexican father.[1]

For three years in the late 1990s, I conducted writing residencies at Adams, increasingly aware of how different the school was from its conservative neighborhood where, ironically, very little Spanish was spoken at all. My role in Adams' English writing classes was ostensibly the same as it had been in other residencies. But I had only to pop my head into the hall to remind myself that the context of my work was decidedly different. There I found kids from kindergarten through sixth grade querying the office staff in Spanish: "*¿Señora, puedo usar el teléfono?*" or "*¿Está la enfermería aquí?*" while classes sang, "*Bate, bate, chocolate,*" a favorite counting song. Why was this so different from other St. Paul residencies, where I would encounter Somali students gossiping in Somali or Hmong students chatting in Hmong? Gradually the answer came clear. The difference stemmed from the fact that while 30 percent of the Adams students (and parents) hailed from Mexico, Puerto Rico, Argentina, Guatemala, Chile, etc., most at Adams were, like Heidi, from Minnesota's Nordic/Germanic majority. Instead of working primarily with students who were seeking (to a certain extent) to subordinate their native language in order to acquire English, I worked at Adams with those who had elected to give Spanish the same precedence as English.

During my three residencies at Adams, I gradually came to understand the philosophy and practice of language-immersion education. Begun in the early 1960s by a group of English-speaking Canadian parents who wanted their children to be schooled in French, the idea of immersion education became established as a viable option in the United States a decade later. Its basic structure continues to be straightforward and compelling. Immediately upon entering kindergarten, students are introduced to the immersion language. (In the case of Adams, the immersion language is Spanish.) By first grade, the immersion language becomes the medium for all instruction in math, geography, science, history, reading, and writing. What this means is that students are taught to read and write for the very first time in a language that, in most cases, is not their native tongue. School instruction in English reading and writing is not introduced until second grade (previously third or fourth) and is integrated into the curriculum one or two periods a day. At upper elementary, the amount of time spent in the immersion language and the dominant language begins to equalize, and if immersion education continues through high school, English accounts for 60 percent and the second language for 40 percent of instruction.[2]

Adams was founded in 1986 by some visionary St. Paul educators, one of whom, Howard Hathaway, was director of world languages for the St. Paul district. Another founder taught Spanish on a local public television station and attracted a following for his innovative techniques. At the time, St. Paul had only one magnet school, but when the community was polled, they voted overwhelmingly to add a Spanish-immersion magnet. Of the Twin Cities, St. Paul has consistently had a slightly larger proportion of Hispanics among its population; furthermore, national interest in south-of-the-border countries and cultures increased the appeal of learning Spanish. From this interest, Adams was born. At first, its two sections of kindergarten and first grade occupied a corner of a much larger school. After three years, Adams became a joint tenant in its current site, the three-story red-brick building with big windows and squeaky floors that I loved. By 1992, Adams had expanded to sixth grade, and its partner, a Montessori program, agreed to vacate to give Adams more room.

The typical Adams parent does not speak Spanish, but appreciates Adams' rich opportunity for language education. As its reputation has grown, Hispanic students from St. Paul's West Side, as well as some political refugees from Central and South American, have attended Adams in greater numbers. The Hispanic students and teachers add their individual accents and linguistic styles to Adams' medley of sounds; they also infuse the curriculum with tangible information about life in Spanish-speaking countries, from Spain itself to Argentina, Peru, Puerto Rico, Mexico, and others.

For some years, Adams also hosted representatives of the animal kingdom: a rabbit named Crayola, a ferret named *Cicatriz* ("Scar"), and assorted gerbils, hamsters, and fish. Gentle-voiced, long-haired librarian John Giese tended the menagerie, along with a wide array of Spanish- and English-language books. The rabbit lasted into my first year at Adams, when common field mice were found consorting with the rabbit for lunch. The other critters moved on more recently. The library, with its huge potted plants, created a rainforest atmosphere, which became one of my favorite places to read students' writing and generally relax.

Since I was teaching in fourth-, fifth-, and sixth-grade English classes, we were discouraged from using Spanish in our poems. Yet the Spanish language and its gestures lurked like a richly endowed if uninvited guest. The message of the school toward language acquisition seemed inclusive rather than exclusive. I, who had spent many challenging hours asking non-English speakers to think, speak, and write in English, now was tantalized by an enlarged mind-set that encompassed not only two languages but many different cultures as well. The students showed every indication of enjoying language play. They spoke bilingually, occasionally throwing in a Spanish word that expressed their meaning better than an English one. They took to metaphor-making with abandon; the room hummed with their alliteration. As they tossed words around, different facets caught the light; they recognized common etymologies in English and Spanish. Often, after a writing session, I congratulated the teachers: "Such fluent writers.

Very sophisticated and curious about words. The students are so at ease with language." Yes, of course they were. They had spent years sampling, tasting, digesting, comparing Spanish and English. This made them not only better writers in English, but far more curious about history and geography than many standard American students.

Teachers from around the world had guided their learning. An exchange teacher from Chile, for instance, who had previously taught in the school, enthusiastically described Pablo Neruda's *Memoirs*.[3] Tossing back her curly red hair, she spoke of Neruda's childhood in Patagonia with its gloomy rainforest; then she sketched for us his adult home on Isla Negra off the coast near Santiago. As we talked of Neruda, a student opened his desk and extracted a Spanish-English edition of Neruda's poems. This prompted me to describe how Minnesota poet Robert Bly had translated and published Neruda in his literary magazine, beginning with *The Fifties*. We then heard the student happily deliver a Neruda ode, first in Spanish, then in English, letting us appreciate how the geography of each language contoured Neruda's celebratory lines.

Another teacher, Concha Fernandez del Rey, began teaching at Adams as an Amity aide from Spain. (The Amity Institute has sponsored foreign teachers or teachers-in-training to work in U.S. schools since 1962.) When she fell in love with an American man, she settled permanently in the Twin Cities and taught fifth grade at Adams. I found Concha's Castilian Spanish, which sounded almost textbook perfect, easier to understand than the hybrid, South American versions that cascaded around the Adams lunchroom, keeping my ears aquiver. Helped by yearly visits to Isla Mujeres near Cancún and my modest knowledge of Italian, I could appreciate and even occasionally understand the rapid, liquid Spanish. Immersion philosophy holds that language acquisition is a natural human process, which children accomplish just as readily as they learn to walk or tie their shoes. With this in mind, Adams plunges English speakers into using Spanish for everything from bathroom breaks to the names of the continents. Then, when students can transfer reading skills from Spanish to English, they acquire grammar in both. Their writing also begins in Spanish and transfers into English, and they often quickly become proficient English readers and writers. Given the philosophy of learning a language through using it, of moving gracefully from simple to more complex lessons, and of exploring both Spanish-language and Anglo-American cultures, I decided that my job at Adams was to give the students a sense of their larger undertaking: an acute sense of how one language (or one people) can influence, challenge, and inspire another.

Francisco Pizarro's knowledge of the Taino (the natives of *Boriquen*, the Taino word for Puerto Rico) provided a rich beginning. The exercise that I developed would require the fourth-graders to imagine Taino history as a series of glances—glances at natural objects, at homes and families, at incoming conquistadores. To assist us, Señor Pizarro, a tall, slim, curly-haired young Puerto Rican, offered a brief crash course in Taino terminology.

- *cacique* the Taino leaders
- *hamaca* hammock
- *bohio* bamboo and straw huts
- *hurricán* a huge wind that blew down trees
- *barracuda* huge predatory fish from the Caribbean

It was surprising how many English words had come from the Taino, probably by way of Spanish. But as is typical with language transmission, once a word entered our language we lost sight of its origin.

To add another layer to our exercise, I introduced Chilean poet Vicente Huidobro to the students. Huidobro, 1893–1948, is renowned for infusing French and Spanish surreal poetry into Chilean literature. Señor Pizarro read Huidobro's poem, "Natural Forces," in Spanish, then in English. Once the class was sufficiently steeped in the Huidobro poem, I initiated a discussion of the word "*mirada*," which the students did not know from their bilingual education. A word that connotes glances, miracles, and marvels, *mirada* can't help but suggest the word "mirror" as well. I wasn't schooled enough in its Spanish connotations to know if they, like the English ones, carried the delightful idea that, as we glance outward with the Huidobro poem, we are also glancing deep into the marvels of imagination. Something to consider while reading "Natural Forces."

Fuerzas naturales

Una mirada

                   para abatir al albatros

Dos miradas

para detener el paisaje
al borde del río

Tres miradas

para cambiar la niña en
volantín

Cuatro miradas

para sujetar el tren que
cae en abismo

Cinco miradas

para volver a encender las estrellas
apagadas por el huracán

Seis miradas

para impedir el nacimiento
del niño acuático

Siete miradas

para prolongar la vida de
la novia

Ocho miradas

para cambiar el mar
en cielo

Nueve miradas

para hacer bailar los
árboles del bosque

Diez miradas

para ver la belleza que se presenta
entre sueño y una catástrofe

Natural Forces

One glance

to knock down the albatross

Two glances

to stop the landscape
at the river's edge

Three glances

to change the girl into
a kite

Four glances

to hold back the train which
falls in the chasm

Five glances

> to relight the stars
> blown out by the hurricane

Six glances

> to prevent the birth
> of the aquatic child

Seven glances

> to prolong the life of
> the bride

Eight glances

> to change the sea
> into sky

Nine glances

> to make the trees in the wood
> dance

Ten glances

> to see the beauty that is present
> between a dream and a catastrophe[4]

The counting structure was so compelling that we decided to incorporate it into our own poems. Much like Wallace Stevens' "Thirteen Ways of Looking at a Blackbird," Huidobro's numbers each announce a new way of looking. To brainstorm for our "*Una mirada*" writing, I suggested that the students draw two circles (like the lenses of a double telescope). Then around the first one, they wrote elements from our discussion of *Boriquen*, such things as masks of mariners with curly beards; gods from Taino mythology; myths of strange white sea birds and sticks that belched fire (guns). On the second circle, I suggested that they list elements from the natural world: times of day, weather, plants, earth forms, bodies of water, anything that might impinge on or color their perception.

It occurred to me that as their poems moved from one glance to the next, their observations could proceed along an anthropological continuum: from nature undisturbed by human life, to the Taino and their island culture, to the Tainos' first glimpse of the Spaniards' ships, to their first beach encounter with these bearded strangers. Since writing the first line of a poem is often the hardest, I made it easy by suggesting that the students combine one item from each circle, letting one of the items act as the narrator. As an example, we put Samuel's first glance on the board. "Una mirada," he wrote, "I, the senna plant, am thrown into the water to stun fish." Though this was supposed to describe the natural world without human life, Samuel obviously had invited a nameless hand into the scene, to scatter the senna over the water's surface. For the second, third, and fourth glances, I encouraged students to focus on things that the Taino used, made, or built. Gina wrote: "Dos miradas, I, the *bohio*, am built of warm bamboo and straw."

For the fifth glance (like the pivotal "five gold rings" in the song "The Twelve Days of Christmas"), I asked the students to create a Taino name for themselves and incorporate it into the line. "Cinco miradas, I, Shell Girl Shining, see big white things that look like big clouds," wrote Liliana. Before concluding with the appearance of Columbus' three ships, we drew the sails and asked ourselves what they looked like. Clouds, leaves, birds, diamonds became incorporated into lines:

> *Seis miradas*, I, Liz master, lie on the beach and see three white objects which I say are only mist, for other than that, I don't know and we could all be wrong. (Niko)

I liked how Niko imagined the Tainos' amazement and their inability to make sense of these new objects. Their surprise carried over into the final "*mirada*" of the poems when the Taino puzzled about the mariners. Lily wrote: "*Seis miradas*, I, Star Moon, ask why they have so many clothes on" and Hannah wrote, "I, the Taino *cacique*, am blinded by the strangers' glistening sharp things." The students impressively conveyed the Tainos' amazement at the strange beings who stepped onto their beach. The Taino compared the new beings and objects to things they knew in their island worlds. Only students who had practiced shifting perspectives from one language to another could have put themselves so readily into the Tainos' place.

Notes on Writing "Una mirada" Poems

Introducing students to Caribbean cultures provides important background for this exercise. We watched a brief video about Caribbean festivals and their blend of many different cultures, from the Native American to the Spanish, Dutch, African, French, English, Portuguese. With a startling syncretism, the festivals combined Native gods with the British Union Jack flag, and African voodoo with blond European faces. These figures danced and sang to an astonishing medley of sounds.

It is also important to talk to students about Caribbean life before the arrival of the Spanish. This is where Señor Pizarro's information was most helpful. We were also aided in our discussion of the Taino by a novel called *Morning Girl*, by Michael Dorris.[5] This novel brings to life the Taino people on the eve of the Spanish arrival. Another helpful book was Francine Jacobs' *The Tainos*,[6] which provided vocabulary, foodstuffs, housing, trade routes, and a brief history of the people. We created Native Taino names for ourselves by blending knowledge of northern Native American naming practices with ideas from Taino culture. In both North and South American traditions, Native American names use elements from the natural world like "White-faced Dolphin" or "Moon Breeze" to evoke a mood or personality trait that will shape the child.[7]

The idea of having an element of nature or culture speak in each line of the poem was inspired by Scott Momaday's poem "The Delight Song of Tsoai-Talee," which begins, "I am a feather on the bright sky" and continues with each line beginning, "I am...". (See the discussion of this poem in Chapter Three of this book.) Like the Momaday poem, Huidobro's "*Una mirada*" poem shifts rapidly from one realm to another. I emphasized that whether a wave or a *hamaca* is speaking, the point of view must remain steady. I found it refreshing to have pre-Spanish Caribbean life told in part from non-human perspectives: from the senna plant which stunned fish, to thunderclouds which brought blinding rain. When we introduced the elements of Taino culture—the *bohio* huts which sheltered from the rain—it was clear how closely related the Taino were to their environment. Beginning with the natural world also prevented the students from personalizing too much and bringing in anachronisms from modern life.

A fine collection of writing by contemporary Puerto Ricans, *Boricuas: Influential Puerto Rican Writings*, provides other suggestive works and information to help shape writing about Caribbean diversity.[8]

II.

In preparing for the sixth-grade portion of my residency, I began to re-search the art of the mask.[9] Just as Huidobro's poem of glances captures the magic of perception and transformation, so masks worldwide portray the excitement and daring of looking through a stranger's face. One glance and we see a lizard whose mouth opens on a frog. In a twinkling of an eye, we peek from inside that lizard to the pulsing throat of the frog we are about to devour. I had visited mask shops on Isla Mujeres, and gazed up at conquis-tadores with flowing beards and pale glass eyes; totem-stack masks of writhing snakes, armadillos, and jaguars; and angel masks with baby-doll faces and wings sprouting from their ears. Imported from all over Mexico, these masks suggested festivals, rituals, games, and tricks, a world full of shamanism and metamorphosis where natural, unpredictable power churned through plant, animal, and human kingdoms. It was not much of a leap to imagine that the Adams students might find in masks a visual equivalent for their amazing leaps between two different languages. What parts of themselves belonged to the Spanish pueblo and what to the English town, to the Taino hurricane and to the English storm? Writing about masks might reach into their psyches and show them how to describe the shifting patterns of their bilingual and bicultural education.

I also knew from personal experience that making masks could cele-brate life-changing experiences. When my father died, I made a mask to honor him. Its demi-globe was covered with spiky feathers and tufts of pa-per printed with his favorite expressions. Working on the mask for months, I glued my sorrow and memories to a face which turned into a mirror of my interior world. I didn't have to wear it to know that it revealed my messy, deeply felt loss.

With the Adams students, I decided to focus on Caribbean and Mexi-can masks, partly because I knew some of these masks firsthand and partly because many of the Hispanic Adams students had ties to Central and South American cultures. In Mayan, Aztec, and other indigenous Ameri-can cultures, I discovered the phenomenon of the double mask. These masks, like many single-visaged ones, played important roles in festivals and religious pageants. My theme would be opposites—opposites that were different like sun/moon, day/night, or opposites that grew out of a common origin, such as clouds and mist or lizards and snakes. To begin, I brought in a sun/moon mask from Mexico and introduced the idea of double-faces. When North Americans say "double-faced," it frequently carries a negative connotation. A double-faced person says one thing, then does another; a double-faced person is disloyal. But, I told my students, in Mayan and Aztec societies, faces sit side by side or on top of each other to deliver extra wallops of power. Hunting societies around the world believe that by donning the faces of their prey, they acquire the animals' cunning and thus stand a better change of outwitting them. Isn't it similar to North American kids who wear devil or monster masks for "trick or treat"? Their little faces are so transformed that we can't help but deliver the goods.

On a more philosophical level, anything desired (think deer or rain) calls forth the animal or plant who needs it to survive (think hungry wolf, parched grass). Thus wolf consumes deer in order to survive, and so on. What may seem like evil to one is good for another. I hoped that students would entertain these philosophical abstractions as they drew on their knowledge of nature's odd pairings: the tiny fish that cleans a whale's back of barnacles or the tropical bird that captures insects in a waterfall. I hoped that my classes would come to appreciate the opposites—pain/joy, red/black, darkness/song, animal/human—and see that these opposites were not simply ideas but were rooted in real-life animal and human dramas.

The Aztec dance for rain, for instance, was performed wearing the dual mask of Xolotl, the god of dualism, fused to his twin Quetzalcoatl. One face wore the rain-petitioning symbols of frog, serpent, beard, and moustache, and the other stuck out a long tongue below bright blue eyes. (In pre-Columbian Aztec society, serpents represented earth and fertility, an important icon in petitioning rain.) In this mask's powerful doubling, opposites were not always what we might expect; serpents and tongues mimicked each other in shape and design, creating a visual kinship.

Other native masks paired animals to compound the wearer's power or to suggest the Lord of the Animals who ruled all animal life. A particularly beguiling set of harvest masks placed human faces in the middle of animal bodies. Worn by dancers celebrating a harvest, these masks suggested that all life rejoiced when the earth gave forth its bounty. Though some cultural meaning associated with these animal masks had been lost, we could suppose that hybrid animals might have represented clan totems or particular experiences of the wearer. I remember a shield made by Humped-wolf, a North American Crow warrior, around 1850.[10] It honored the warrior's survival during a blizzard when he crawled inside a buffalo carcass to stay warm. Inside the buffalo, he dreamed about a bull buffalo urinating to mark its territory. Later he put this image on a shield to retain its power. Perhaps the buffalo image told of his gratitude for survival and for all the material things the buffalo gave his people.

Masks in Hispanic America also displayed evidence of cultural layering. Under the influence of Spanish Catholicism, pre-Columbian tiger masks were transformed into devils with horns and were worn in festivals by rascals who taunted people in power. Such syncretism, to use the anthropological term, expressed how a conquered people used images from their conquerors to undercut their oppression in sly ways. I hoped that examples of such transformation would inspire the Adams students to layer in their masks the many shifts of culture, power, and language that had crossed the Americas.

Gradually, as I studied many different kinds of masks, I decided to take a rather bold tack. Instead of having all the sixth-graders at Adams create two-faced masks that represented different parts of their personalities, I suggested to some that the dual faces represent on one side South American culture and on the other side something from the United States. The general plan that emerged was to have students design their own double masks, then write poems in which each side of the mask spoke. Glimpsing the risks—the poems turning into bare litanies of facts, or diatribes against countries—I emphasized that the poems must symbolize and compress like good poems, and perhaps use humor to entertain the reader. I also implied that the double masks might tap into the sixth-graders' delight in challenging authority and social prescriptions. If they pooh-poohed the idea of contrasting countries, maybe they'd be intrigued by conflicts within themselves. Whatever they chose, I had to recognize that their motives and ideas had to be their own.

Previous years had taught me that Adams sixth-graders could write marvelous things, but of course each class and year was different. In the several years since I first taught at the school, its character had changed. More Hispanic students were enrolled. This meant that classes contained more firsthand knowledge than before about Latin American countries. But would the students read and write English as well as earlier classes? Would some of them find it easier to write in Spanish than in English? As the students began to draw and write, I walked around the room to see what was happening.

As with many other classes embarking on unfamiliar projects, drawing made a good place to start because it was preverbal and it gave students concrete images that they could describe in words. The Adams drawings were wonderfully inventive: the Mayan twin gods, Xolotl/Quetzalcoatl, sported lizards and a winged devil on their bearded heads; a Mayan/American wore a crew cut on one side and a flowing Mohawk and earring on the other. There was a dog/cat, a moon/star, a criminal/student, and a scary/scared mask with huge rays for evil hair. One of my favorites was earth/sea. Mother Earth was depicted as a flowering tree with a huge eye where the branches joined the trunk, and the Sea was scalloped with waves where fish swam around one bloodshot eye. Some students drew vivid shapes with expressive shading; others presented more schematic cartoons; a few drew nothing. The more motivated of the non-drawers made lists of contrasting words. The rest fidgeted or looked off into space. I tried not to worry, realizing that, for some kids, drawing is intimidating. I hoped that they would eventually find something of interest and try writing a poem.

Some drawings had more verve than the accompanying poems, but that wasn't the case with Mary's big, egg-shaped Rainy Season/Dry Season. The egg-shaped mask wore delicate leaves of hair twining into twigs; the lower face was crossed by raindrops which fell among dying corn plants. Gaia-like, Rainy Season/Dry Season sailed through space, carrying her own atmosphere. The accompanying poem provided a study in contrasts: wet/dry; English/Spanish.

I am

Yo soy

Rainy season

Temporada seco

Wet

seco

cool

      caliente

The same

      pero differente

together

      pero separados

leafy green

      secco sin ni un hoja

alive

      y muerto

golden flowers

      ya no está

now I'm here

      ahora va.

On the back of her sheet, Mary had written a slightly different version of the poem, entirely in English except for the last five lines.

Dry

      wet

hot

      cool

The same

      yet different

together

      yet apart

leafy green

      dry and bare

dead

      and alive

golden flowers

      ya no está

ha ora está

      now I'm here

Now I will leave

      ahora va.

I didn't have a chance to ask Mary about her use of two languages and her reason for creating a second version of the poem. I sensed that in the first poem, the Spanish spoke a dry, killing message, bare and uneventful, and in the second, she changed the climates to allow English to try out a different rhythm of presentation. Also intriguing was the ending—"*ahora va*"—saying in Spanish what English had just said. It appeared important to her that Spanish have the last word in this second version, a kind of complement to its harsher message in the first version. Though I suspected that Mary had worked quickly and intuitively, it seemed that she was experimenting with different mixes and textures of the two languages, each evoking potentially different feelings about her life, its seasons, and her bilingual development. But maybe she had written the second version as a kind of translation, being considerate of me, a non-Spanish speaker. Or maybe she was covering herself from the charge that she should be writing in English during English class. I judged that Mary was a native Spanish speaker who had learned to read and write in Spanish. But given the school philosophy, she could just as likely have been a very bright native English speaker who employed Spanish with gusto.

Another startling poem was unsigned but titled "The People of Our Villa."

> Beautiful
> Uruguay
> dying seals on *isla de lobos*
> Ugly
> Long peninsula
> Mountains   Short
> Different in many ways
> Excited—bulging grapefruits
> People calm
> Positive—Peace talks
> Wars—negative
> Happy
> Sad
> Sharing many emotions
> Revealing
> concealing
> Mature
> childish
> two sides to every person
> Crying

> laughing
> Losing
> finding
> everything will be wonderful someday
> Man
> Woman
> Rich
> Poor

Now, several years later, I don't know which class produced this poem. I had given one class the assignment to address different Spanish American countries. Maybe the author was a Uruguayan student displaced by war. The poem's anonymity made me sad because I could not locate the student to ask about the poem. (Classroom teachers almost always remember students vividly, even after three or four years.) Was the student ashamed of revealing kernels of pain, the dying seals that marked a sick country? Humbled because I had not expected a student to pour out grief and anguish in this exercise, I sensed a life stretched taut from one hemisphere to another, walking a tightrope but unsure if anyone would catch the fall. This was a sobering reminder that poetry writing for young people is not simply word play or tossing off an assignment. Like all poetry, students' writing can suddenly turn deadly earnest, calling up sharp expressions of pain or joy.

In Richard Wilbur's poem "The Writer," his daughter is typing in the room above him, and the poet initially wishes her "a lucky passage." When her typing stops a long time, then furiously resumes, he evokes a trapped starling who beats itself against ceiling and wall until finally it

> ... lifted off from a chair-back,
> Beating a smooth course for the right window
> And clearing the sill of the world.

He apologized to his daughter:

> It is always a matter, my darling,
> Of life or death, as I had forgotten. I wish
> What I wished you before, but harder.[11]

I hoped I had not romanticized the students' work or trivialized the difficulty of its creation.

As I continued to leaf through my folder of mask poems, trying to quiet my distress about things I could never know for sure, I encountered a drawing of a dark-bearded Spaniard embracing a statuelike Incan face. The drawing captured exactly what I'd hoped would happen for some students: masks as double images of stranger and native, conqueror and conquered. The poem, by a student named Desiree, slipped quickly into two different voices:

> *Los españoles*
> >The Spaniards
> >Trying to take over our land
> *Los incas*
> >The Incas
> >Keeping us from finding *oro* and *plata*
> We want to keep our
> land and culture
> >We want to capture them
> >And make them our slaves
> We are at peace with nature
> >We want to expand our territory.

Though expressing contrary political attitudes had not been a conscious assignment for the class, the masks we had studied made plain that the native peoples often did not welcome the Spanish invasion. Spanish colonialism had been followed by United States interference with the economics and politics of Central and South America. The students were, perhaps, more aware of this than I.

Notes on Drawing Masks and Writing Mask Poems

Introducing students to masks around the world set the stage for concentration on masks from Central and South America. I showed a video about masks from the Minneapolis Institute of Art, then asked students to take notes on elements from the masks that intrigued them. From these notes grew conversations about the purpose of various kinds of masks. Each class spent a session studying and talking about masks, including the double-faced masks from Central and South America.

The model for their poems came from Paul Fleischman's book of

poems in two voices, *Joyful Noise*.[12] (See Chapter Five for
Fleischman's poem "Grasshoppers," which I used with Adams and
other students.) When two students read the poem "Grasshoppers"
aloud, their different voices emphasized the poem's play with dualism. Ideas, sentences, even words split apart between the voices,
and repetition traded back and forth to create a songlike quality.
Each voice also seemed to express a different tone or experience
from the other. When it came time to write, I encouraged students
to create a poem in two voices for their two-faced masks. Essen-
tially, each side of the mask would speak, describing, emoting, remembering, etc.

We brainstormed lists before shaping the poems. This helped students put words and ideas to what they had drawn. I usually let inspiration for such lists arise from our content and process. Here, the
suggestions were to list the features of the masks; then what each
half-face remembered, thought, wished for; then what each face
might say to the other face. For the classes that created masks about
different Central and South American countries, I gathered picture
books about relevant countries and let each student select one or
two books. This gave the writers material and images to use in de-
signing their two-faced masks. These books from the school library
added bits of politics, economics, history, festivals, geography, food,
natural environment, etc., to the poems.

III.

Nobel Peace Prize–winner Rigoberta Menchú (born in 1959) is an outstanding hero of indigenous resistance, and her autobiography, *I, Rigoberta
Menchú: An Indian Woman in Guatemala*,[13] provides vivid details of Mayan life. As often as possible, I try to broaden students' knowledge of different people, hoping that details from past eras or far-flung cultures will
extend their sympathy and invigorate their poems. Sometimes the lessons
come close to home, as a class listens to how an elder goofed up as a kid.
This can soothe a kid who's gotten in trouble and turn shame into laughter.
When the lessons come from faraway, American students may discover
that other lives are much harder than their own. This can make young people grateful for their own modest abundance. Once students make a

stranger's story their own, I don't have to use the word *tolerance*. The students have given their affectionate acceptance, almost without knowing it.

As I considered what should follow the mask exercise at Adams, I remembered my own thrilled first encounter with Rigoberta Menchú. Her autobiography, rendered in simple, compelling language, offered broad strokes of history and geography to paint the portrait of a people often in poverty. She drew startling descriptions of marriage and birthing practices, the strong value placed on community support for a mother and child, and a Mayan baby's early preparation for life's harsh lessons. Her heroism in organizing against workers' mistreatment by multinational corporations and against damage done to native culture by the Guatemalan civil war commanded attention. Since I wanted to introduce students to writing from both a landscape and a portrait perspective, I elected to reduce the long lens of the mask exercise, which had zoomed out to describe an entire culture, and train it close-up on the complexities of individuals within a culture. Though the mask exercise had been successful, I knew it was time to introduce my students to a native of the region that we had been studying.

Asking around, I quickly discovered an aide whose husband was Guatemalan; it turned out that he was from the same Kiche Mayan tribe as Menchú herself. As I thought about inviting him to speak to the sixth-grade classes, I reasoned that he would provide a far more accurate link to Rigoberta Menchú's childhood than I could, from my book reading and one-time visit to Guatemala. Federico Ajpop was a slender young man who had lived in Minnesota for approximately five years. He seemed at ease with the classes, and his stories brought the Guatemalan Altiplano [Western Highlands] alive. Alternating elegantly between English and Spanish, Federico began by describing Guatemala's twenty-five languages. (The United States has more than 300 languages, but Guatemala is only about the size of Tennessee.) "Twenty-two of our twenty-five languages are Mayan," Federico smiled, "one is Español, one is Xinca, one Garifuna." Mayan, as a term, defines native people who inhabit what is now the Mexican Yucatán and Guatemala. Just as a number of different dialects developed within the Iroquois nation in North America, so Mayans with different dialects were joined in a loose confederation that declined around 1200 A.D. "In my language, *maiz* is *Ixim*." Corn, or *maiz* in Spanish, was the first word Federico taught us and this suggested how crucial *Ixim* continues to be for the Mayan people. Fleetingly, I wondered what would be the first English word we would teach a stranger, but I didn't want to interrupt Federico to ask the students. As Federico talked, he offered us details of his own life, giving us a very personal vocabulary lesson. "My family were weavers," Federico told us, "*tejedores*. In Mayan our village is called 'At the top of hot water' because hot springs are found above us in the mountains; *Chuimegena* in Mayan; in Spanish is it *Totonicapan*."

Federico drew a map of Guatemala and identified his town. Occasionally he mentioned the civil war, which surprised me because I had thought he was too young to have experienced it. The students were enthralled, but not by the war. They were fascinated by his intimate introduction to Mayan culture. They chimed in: "What are some similarities among all the Mayan people in your country?" In response, Federico smiled his gentle, white-toothed smile and said simply, "Two seasons, rainy and dry. We all eat tamales. And all believe in our common origin: *Yumkax* [the Mayan deity of agriculture] mixed corn with blood to make people." It seemed, from what he told us, that his family led a typical Mayan life; his mother ground corn and many of his friends' families had worked in the *fincas* in the lowlands. "*Fincas*" are large plantations owned by outsiders, often United States corporations. Rigoberta and her family had also worked in the *fincas*, forced to this by necessity. "The living conditions were not good," Federico continued. "Many people were packed in small rooms." Here, in this crowded environment far from her home in the Altiplano, Rigoberta had begun her political education. At age five, she had glimpsed economic oppression by watching her mother work to exhaustion:

> My mother ... often had food ready at three o'clock in the morning for the workers who started work early, and at eleven she had the food for the midday meal ready. At seven in the evening she [made] food for the group. In between times, she worked picking coffee to supplement what she earned. ... That's when my consciousness was born. ... I wanted to work, more than anything to help her.[14]

I commented that Rigoberta later worked to rouse native Mayan people to protest these harsh conditions. Without appearing to hear me, the students immediately took the focus back to Federico: "Tell about the war," called a boy. Federico, with his sad smile, explained that his family had lived close to a big city of 100,000 people and thus were not so seriously affected by the war as Rigoberta and her family. Pausing for a moment as if testing something, Federico finally said that he had been aware of the war, but not involved in it. Again he paused. I imagined that since the war had been sparked in part by American companies, he did not want to offend us. When he resumed speaking, he explained that since the war had not touched his area, he had been able to go to school in the nearby city and then, because of his good grades, to continue at a boarding school, forty miles away. Explaining the war to us, he said,

> In Guatemala, eighty percent of the land was owned by six percent of the people, usually outsiders or international companies. When the Guatemalan government decided they must either tax the land or buy some of it back, the companies put a low price on it, hoping to avoid paying high taxes. But the government understood what they were doing and bought the land at these low prices. This angered many U.S. legislators. Through the CIA, the U.S. government encouraged many exiled Guatemalan military men to return. Once they did, they attacked the government, and fighting began. From 1961 to 1990, we had civil war.

We were all stunned by his clear rendition of these disturbing events. I was not sure how many of the students understood the intricate economic and military maneuverings, but like me, they hung onto Federico's words, eager to learn how he had fared during the war and why he had left Guatemala. At this point, we had forgotten about Rigoberta; we wanted to know the fate of this young man in front of us.

Federico had come to the United States like this: In Guatemala, he had been teaching Spanish and studying to become a lawyer. His wife, Denise, who had traveled from Minnesota to study Spanish, had enrolled in the very school where he taught. When they became friends and decided to marry, they chose, in 1997, to move to the United States. Now they lived in St. Paul, where Denise worked at Adams as an aide, and Federico roofed houses. "I cannot use my Guatemalan education here," he said, smiling ruefully. "But, you know, it was my choice to come to the U.S." His situation reminded me of many immigrants. For example, Dr. Jama, the Somali

Ph.D. who was an aide at Como High School, had been highly trained in Somalia and Italy, but he could not use his expertise here because his training did not fit U.S. patterns. I thought such situations were a shame. Federico, in a similar quandary, could not teach or practice law in the U.S. His story, brought to us with his quiet, unassuming charm, did not express resentment, but understanding. By now, we had left Rigoberta behind, and Federico had become the center of our lesson. This was clear evidence of the power of a personal testament. Like many Adams students, he was living a multilanguage identity: Spanish was his second language, and now he was speaking English.

The emotional quality of Federico's visit proved to be a wonderful impetus for the ballads which I had chosen as our creative response to Federico's story. The following day, we discussed ballads as long poems that tell stories in multiple verses. We put phrases from Federico's oral history on the board, and I mentioned a bit more about Rigoberta. The students were far more interested in Federico than in her, and I was grateful that, like her account, his had expanded beyond his own individual life to consider the traditions and trials of the Mayan people. It was appropriate that the students wanted to use some of Federico's communal phrases as choruses for the ballad: "Twenty-two Mayan languages/yet they speak the same story" or "They took our language, our smiles, our song/They gave our town a different name" or "High in the mountains, warm and cool/In Mayan our town means 'at the top of hot water.'" In ballads, choruses carry general attitudes and expand the meaning of individual verses.

From these early suggestions, we wove a series of class-choruses, and each student wrote a verse. We discussed how verses should advance a narrative or provide a series of vignettes, all related to the central theme articulated in the chorus. Choruses repeated in a chantlike manner their summary or exemplary lines, and sometimes the ends of choruses changed to suggest changes in the story.

> Chorus One:
> Town in Guatemalan mountains
> Town called *Chuimegena*
> On top of hot springs
> Kiche Mayan town

Verse One:
Muchas animales
Kiche, Español
Perros—tzi—dogs follow
People into high fields

Chorus Two:
Town in the mountains
Town of hot springs

Verse Two:
Ajpop family weave palms
Into mats for quilting
Named pop, ajpop of mats

Chorus Three:
Kiche town speak
One of 22 Mayan languages
Town of hot springs

Verse Three:
Muchas ropas
Hand-woven *Guipil*
Vivid patterns different
For each town, an array of colors

Chorus Four:
Town of the Mayans, mountain with hot springs
Volcanos everywhere

Verse Four:
Yumkax, old lady of corn
Tried making humans
From wood, from clay
Only mixing blood with corn
Brought humans to life.

The ballads, more thematic than storytelling, contained a blend of Spanish, English, and Mayan from Federico's Kiche Mayan story. This mix of languages came to represent the political and historic relations among the different elements of Federico's culture. English stood for the United States and the language that we all spoke, but it also represented an element in a power struggle played out in Guatemala. Spanish stood for Adams' teaching goal and the story of Guatemala's invasion and rule by the Spanish. Mayan represented the oldest language in Guatemala's history, and the traditions that Federico and Rigoberta wanted to preserve and protect. Quite a bit for a brief ballad to carry. (For a discussion of the ballad-writing process with a class, see *The Story in History*, pp. 61–68.)

The Adams Spanish Immersion residencies allowed me and the students to revel in new knowledge: from Caribbean festivals and worldwide masks to *Boriquen* history to Rigoberta Menchú's and Federico Ajpop's memories of the Guatemalan highlands to another visitor's extraordinary description of the Mexican floating gardens of Teotihuacan (stuff for another sixth-grade ballad). Never before had I rung quite so many changes so quickly on new material and combinations. Never before had other teachers offered such startling and pertinent information. The results were gratifying, full of discovery, adaptation, and collaboration.

Ultimately, no language or culture has solved every one of life's challenges. Learning how languages differ in the value they give things or in their ability to express certain feelings or experiences translates into a vast array of historical, geographic, economic encounters. How wonderful that learning another language can initiate students into the heart of another culture! Giving a language other than the dominant one preeminence in a school also shifts the attention away from the more strident (and, in the U.S., more commercial) messages of the dominant U.S. culture and toward more fundamental awareness of how culture works in general, what people value, and how they weave work and play together.[15]

NOTES

[1]Heidi Bernal drew me to Adams initially and helped bring me back. Ours was a most pleasant association as she was finishing her master's degree at Hamline University during my stay, and we could talk about our common ground in high education as well as our Adams Spanish Immersion art and writing projects. Her master's in education thesis topic at Hamline was "Supporting Emergent Literacy in a Spanish Immersion Kindergarten Program," 1999. Heidi is now ELL supervisor for the St. Paul Public Schools.

[2]Due to concern that immersion students might fall behind their peers, numerous comprehensive tests have been conducted over the years. They have consistently shown that "Immersion students do as well or better than their monolingual peers in the subject areas

tested." (Marguerite Ann Snow, *Immersion Teacher Handbook*. University of California Center for Language Education and Research, 1987, pp. 9–10.) Moreover, tested in the immersion language, immersion students fare far better than students who have studied the target language as a foreign language only one period a day. It is also true that from the day they enter school, Adams students score very high in the gifted and talented index, which suggests that many come from highly literate environments. Many already read English before they enter Adams for kindergarten.

[3]Pablo Neruda, *Memoirs*, translated by Hardie St. Martin (Penguin, 1992).

Pablo Neruda, *Selected Poems: A Bilingual Edition*, edited by Nathaniel Tarn, translated by Anthony Kerrigan, W. S. Merwin, Alastair Reid, Nathaniel Tarn (Delta/Dell Publishing Company, 1972).

In the late 1980s, when I was teaching through a COMPAS extended-residency program called Dialogue, I met Darlene Kunze, ESL teacher at Harding High, who had a college minor in Spanish and had lived in South America for a while. With her and an Argentine friend Norma Avendik, I worked on translating some Mexican poets whose books I had bought in Cancún. Buying two volumes of Neruda with many translators was an education in translators' variety as we worked to sharpen our skills.

[4]Vicente Huidobro, "Fuerzas naturales," translated by David Ossman and Carlos Hagan, *The Selected Poetry of Vicente Huidobro*, edited by David M. Guss (New Directions, 1991).

[5]Michael Dorris, *Morning Girl* (Hyperion, 1992).

[6]Francine Jacobs, *The Tainos* (Putnam Juvenile, 1992).

[7]*Shaking the Pumpkin: Traditional Poetry of the Indian North Americas*, edited by Jerome Rothernberg (Bantam Doubleday Dell, 1971; revised edition, University of New Mexico, 1991). This excellent sampling of all kinds of chants, rituals, poetry, and naming practices has guided my teaching and thinking about Native American history with words. It contains many sections about naming people, months, experiences.

[8]*Boricuas: Influential Puerto Rican Writings*, edited by Roberto Santiago (Ballantine, 1995). Heidi Bernal gave me the book as a good-bye present at my last residency.

I've also used *The Penguin Book of Caribbean Verse in English*, edited by Paula Burnett (Viking Penguin, 1986).

[9]Donald Cordry, *Mexican Masks* (University of Texas Press, 1980). The vivid photographs and excellent text made this my major resource for the mask residency at Adams.

[10]Humped-wolf, "Shield," illustrated and discussed in Evan Mauer, Louise Lincoln, George P. Horse Capture, David W. Penney, Father Peter J. Powell, catalogue for the exhibition *Visions of the People* (The Minneapolis Institute of Art, 1992, p. 125).

[11]Richard Wilbur, "The Writer." *Collected Poems, 1943–2004* (Harcourt, 2004, p. 128).

[12]Paul Fleischman, *Joyful Noise: Poems for Two Voices* (HarperCollins Children's Books, 1992).

[13]Rigoberta Menchú, *I, Rigoberta Menchú: An Indian Woman in Guatemala*, edited and introduced by Elisabeth Burgos-Debray, translated by Ann Wright (Verso, 1983, 1984).

[14]Ibid, p. 34.

[15]In trying to grasp a number of difficult subjects related to immersion education and second-language learning, I identified several areas about which I wanted more knowledge: educational policies and politics surrounding immersion education, research about student achievement in immersion programs, and the changing awareness of students' difficulties learning to read in a second language. Heidi Bernal, during my residencies at Adams, loaned me a number of books that she was using for her master's degree thesis on immersion education. They are:

Nancy Cloud, Fred Genesee, Else Hamayan. *Dual Language Instruction: A Handbook for Enriched Education* (Heinle & Heinle Publishers, 2000).

Helena Curtain and Carol Ann Bjornstand Pesola, *Languages and Children, Making the Match: Foreign Language Instruction for an Early Start, Grades K–8, Second Edition* (New York: Longman, 1994).

Immersion Education: International Perspectives, edited by Robert Keith Johnson and Merrill Swain (Cambridge University Press, 1997).

Darlene Kunze also gave me many materials about second-language acquisition. These included:

A workshop bibliography by Stephen D. Krashen about his new research in ELL up to 2000 and a keynote address by Elaine Tarone and Diane Tedick, University of Minnesota, "Conversations with Mainstream Teachers: What can we tell them about second language learning and teaching?" (Both presented at the MinneTESOL conference, November 10, 2000.) From annotated bibliographies compiled by these speakers, I noted the following:

Susan Bosher and Jenise Rowekamp, "The Refugee/Immigrant in Higher Education: The Role of Educational Background" (*College ESL* 8, 1:23, 1998).

Jim Cummin, "Language Proficiency, Bilingualism, and Academic Achievement," in *Bilingualism and Special Education: Issues in Assessment and Pedagogy* (College Hill Press, 1984, pp. 130–151). Also Jim Cummin, "Second Language Acquisition within Bilingual Education Programs." In *Issues in Second Language Acquisition: Multiple Perspectives* (Newbury House, 1988).

David Ramirez, Sandra Yuen, and Dena Ramey, *Longitudinal Study of Structured English Immersion Strategy, Early-Exit and Late-Exit Transitional Bilingual Education Programs for Minority Language Children: Final Report*, vols. 1 and 2 (Acquirre International, 1991).

Lily Wong-Fillmore. "When Learning a Second Language Means Losing the First," *Early Childhood Research Quarterly* (6, 1991, pp. 323–346).

CHAPTER FIVE

Centerpoint and "High Falls" Elementary Schools: Poems in Two Voices

Dear Marcos, let my words
of poetry pierce your mind
and heart:
Camel, oh camel, stubborn as
heck, eating leaves off
the tree with its long
*neck. Sniffing its **san***
*and swinging its **seen**, the good*
old camel is the opposite
of mean.

—Greg O., fifth grade
[Note: A camel's *san* is "nose"; his *seen* is "tail."]

I.

In 2004, Farah Nur (an immigrant Somali poet) and I found ourselves at a school called Centerpoint Elementary, a magnet charter school in the northern suburbs of St. Paul. Sharing a low brick building with a more traditional elementary school, Centerpoint softened the stiff cold of January outside into a view of dark pines stretching toward big White Bear Lake. Each fourth/fifth-grade classroom centered around carpeted risers where students met for morning sessions. This magnet school had been founded by parents to exemplify high parental involvement; multi-age, nongraded, noncompetitive classrooms; and theme-based, multicultural education. Now, after more than fifteen years, the philosophy worked beautifully: parents dedicated forty hours a year, and the experienced staff worked constantly on perfecting their team-teaching approach.

Farah and I were going to add poetry writing to a three-year collaboration that Centerpoint had initiated with a school I will call "High Falls," a Minneapolis charter school begun by Somali and Oromo parents. In this brave and successful pairing, students exchanged letters and journal entries, visited each others' classrooms, and (best of all) went sledding, a comparatively new experience for the African students. Centerpoint's suburban, largely white, middle-class kids were very curious about their High Falls counterparts, born mostly in the Horn of Africa and speaking several African languages. "Kids look immediately for common ground," said Centerpoint teacher John Leininger. "By being together, they learn that commonalities are more important than differences." But differences there were. To envision High Falls, imagine the snowy Mississippi River where the school was housed in a former post office near the tumble of St. Anthony Falls.

As I would soon realize, High Falls was an astonishing experiment. Founded several years before by Somali and Oromo parents disturbed by their children's treatment in public schools, the school was governed by the parents' desire that their children's American-style education remain true to their Somali and Oromo beliefs and cultures.[1] The school had hired young American teachers to work with aides who spoke the African languages. It was with both excitement and anxiety that I approached the responsibility of teaching an immigrant people about their own poetry.

As we began to prepare for the residency, I learned from Farah that poetry had been an integral part of traditional Somali life, contributing to work, festivals, and weddings; it also was one medium for the retelling of clan history. In Somalia's oral culture, a hallmark of its nomadic population, poetry had developed a vibrant declamatory style. Poems often began by addressing a relative or friend; refrains of single lines built rhythm and choral energy. Somali poets also emphasized alliteration, threading lines and ideas together to make a poem easier to memorize. Some poems even commented on this technique. In this oral culture, poetry quickly became the property of the people; those with quick memories were valued as reciters of poems. When battery-powered tape recorders came on the scene, urban and rural Somalis took to them immediately. They were perfect for keeping abreast of the latest poetic duels. In fact, observers claimed that the civil war in Somalia had been inflamed by taped readings of such duels.

Even though these duels were outlawed by President Siad Barre, a clandestine poetic revolution kept turning out tapes that contributed to Barre's overthrow in 1991.[2]

"We say, 'Whenever you find camels, you will find Somalis,'" Farah told the Centerpoint students as he smiled and drew a map of Somalia on the board. The country looked like a spear pointing into the Gulf of Aden on the north and the Indian Ocean on the south. He colored in the zones of Somalian ecology: tropical green along the ocean, semi-arid thorn bush inland, and mountains on the north. "When it rains, there is green," he said; "otherwise, the grass and trees lose their leaves just as in Minnesota winter." After this conversation on the carpeted bleachers at Centerpoint, the fourth/fifth-grade students took big sheets of paper to their desks and began drawing camels. Whatever else we did, Farah and I had agreed that we had to write camel poems. The camel is to Somali poetry what the skylark is to the English lyric or snow is to the Minnesota pioneer saga. Plus, children are instinctively drawn to animals. Camels, with their haughty, stately gait, would lead the Centerpoint students into the Somali thorn bush.

Somali camels are tall with one hump, Farah emphasized, not short with two humps like Arabian camels. Somali camels have long necks; they can go a month without water. "Wow," cried the kids. "We could go a month without water, right?"

"No," corrected John, their teacher. "We'd die after three days without water. We could go a month without food."

As the children reveled in their drawings, Farah and I read aloud from a wonderful camel poem, "Where True Profit Lies," by Cumar Xuseen "Ostreeliya." The students and I were quite surprised to learn that Farah was related to the author: "My father's uncle, and a seafarer," Farah mentioned demurely. The beautiful last name ("Ostreeliya") was apparently an addendum meant to commemorate the time he had spent in Australia. It also suggested how rarely someone from Somalia reached distant Australia, with its own batch of fascinating animals.

Before reading from his relative's poem, with the students chomping at the bit, Farah took time to discuss some subtle aspects of Somali poetry. First and foremost, he informed us that Somali poems frequently begin with the author addressing a friend. The gait of the poem is leisurely, as if addressing a group resting after a day's trek in the bush. The concerns of traditional poetry are those of everyday nomadic life (or, more recently, urban situations). Using expansive rhythms and emphatic sounds, the poet proclaims a subject in a wide and general sense, then moves in close to describe small intimate details well known to the audience. This is a poetry of celebration, reminiscent of Walt Whitman, with a loving piling up of details. Traditional metaphors refer to rain or drought, trees or moon, camels and milk, and love is expressed as a close kinship tie. Though Farah did not emphasize this, traditional Somali poetry has also been gender specific: more often written by men, it is also the province of women, who have used drums to accompany their works.

Listening to him, I imagined that Somali poetry treasured the people's common experiences, emphasizing the shared values of strength and kinship. For every Somali, owning camels had been a sign of prosperity. That is exactly what Farah's kinsman declaimed:

> When I turn my mind to the fibers of poetry, Maxamed, to their
> very core,
> My sound-matching words have never failed to create a worthy
> heritage.
> Even in my childhood I have already learnt the art of their
> composition ...
> . . . .
> The care of sheep and goats—that's work for women and their
> children
> ... there's glistening milk and buttermilk in plenty
> When the fresh grass sprouts in the *karan* rains ...
> But when drought comes, horned beasts will perish, that is
> certain.
> O you who tend ewes!
> Remember, it's in camel-rearing that true profit lies.
>
> A man distressed and hungry in the cold of the rainless season
> Has only to taste the milk that issues, faintly sour,
> From the udders of a camel
> For him soon to feel there is a place deep in his body
> Which has received comfort and solace.
> . . . .

The she-camels may have stayed for months in the Hawd
    bushland,
They may have fed only on *suud* acacia pods and winding
    meygaag plants,
Yet here they are, each one in calf, each beautiful and thriving!
. . . .
... at dawn
The camels throng at the thorny gate of their pen. ...
And as [the camels] get near the water they utter cries of longing.
The milch-camels now need wait no longer
After the hard time they have spent without salty water ...
. . . .
The camels now have had their fill
And on a grassy spot they are made to rest.
. . . .
A Somali may gather great wealth,
Diamonds he may have and horses too,
He may even wear clothes of wool or fine white cloth
And sport a splendid turban—
But he has no legacy to leave behind him
Unless he rears the beasts whose necks bear wooden bells
. . . .
Call the camels! Call the camels!
A man who has reared no camels will always be a pauper.
         —Cumar Xuseen "Ostreeliya"[3]

It had been a long time since Farah had seen Somali camels. Born in
1968, he had escaped the Somali civil war in 1991 by going to Kenya. Later,
he acquired a degree in English literature from Augustana College, University of Alberta, Canada. Farah knew American life (icebox variety) inside
out. When he read the camel poem to the students, his infectious warmth
sparkled with teacherly glee: "Do you know how thirsty a camel can be after
thirty days without water? They get uppity and kick if you withhold water
from them." He swung his leg back and viciously swung it forward with a
practiced soccer kick.

"Have you ever been kicked, Farah?" I cried, imagining the power of a
camel's kick.

"No, not me, but my brother. He was watering camels at our grandfather's trough. A camel fetched him a hard kick and broke his kneecap." Before long, Farah found himself writing down the camel's anatomical vocabulary in Somali:

- Camel: *Geel*
- Hump: outer part: *Tuur*; inner spongy part: *Kuros*
- Legs: *Lugo*
- Milk: *Caano*
- Belly: *Calool*
- Neck: *Luqun*
- Head: *Madax*
- Nose: *San*
- Tail: *Seen*
- Ear: *Dhag*
- Eye: *Il*; Eyes: *Indho*
- Eyelashes: *Tiribo*
- Baby She-Camel: *Nirig*
- Baby He-Camel: *Qurbar*

As he wrote, Farah explained that camels' tongues are long, black, and calloused, good for eating thorny bush. Their milk is slightly salty and sour. As he said the Somali word for milk, "*caano*," he dropped his jaw for the double *a*, as if letting milk spread invitingly over his tongue. "Camels love salt. The herder takes them to areas spread with crusted salt, and the camels nibble, nibble." His fingers nibbled in the air. We laughed. "'Ships of the desert,' we call camels because they carry all kinds of burdens. The big stud camels are in the lead," he explained. One of the students called out the word *caravan*. "Yes," Farah nodded enthusiastically, "they are roped together in long caravans. Some herders own hundreds of camels. The milch camels carry smaller loads, and baby camels walk beside their mothers." A hot desert land had filled the classroom with thorn trees rising toward the camels' hungry mouths.

As with any typical fourth- or fifth-grade class, quiet writing time didn't last long. In his easygoing way, Farah helped subdue less productive children by sitting next to them and encouraging them. I also went from desk to desk, but my energy was more propulsive than his. By now, we had established a good rapport: Farah was the jovial storyteller, and I the directive administrator. His expansive, friendly manner, his easy settling into companionship, his slightly formal address: all reminded me of my Italian-American father. As Dr. Jama had told me when I had worked with Somali and Oromo students several years before at Como Senior High School, parts of Somalia had been under Italian rule for many years.

Farah had been late the first day (winter car-trouble), but he entered the second day with a bevy of plastic camels he had borrowed from the High Falls office. The camels were a huge hit. Farah immediately pointed out details that we had missed the previous day. Camels have huge teeth. "They spit when they are angry," Farah informed us. Also, their front legs bend back at the knee, unlike human legs. This allows the very tall animals to bed down easily in the sand, lowering back feet first. Such surprises, along with the fun of new Somali camel words, fueled the students' delight in writing their camel poems. Almost effortlessly, they captured the easy gait of the Somali poem:

> Dear Jeanne,
> This poem will interest you.
> Did you know that when a camel is born
> it is four feet tall? When they are full grown
> they are seven feet tall. They call it the ship
> in the sand. That they have a black tongue.
> Milk tastes salty and sour. The camels
> in Somalia are like money to us.
>   —Isabella G.

> Oh, Connor, let me tell
> you of the wonders of the camel.
> The *il* [eye] of the camel
> is like a dark pebble on the beach
> The camel is floating
> above the earth.
> Its throat is dying
> of thirst.
> The tail is like
> a sharp needle pointing down
> The hump like
> a beautiful sunset
> The hooves shoot across

> the hot sand
> The refreshing water
> going down its throat
> The color of the camel
> as tan as the beautiful sand
> The power of the kick
> will knock you
> out. The feeling
> of anger passes through
> when there is no water.
> —Gavin D.

Many of the students created wonderful comparisons: "organ-pipe *lugo*" [legs] and "hump like a beautiful sunset." But, more powerfully, they honored the Somali poetic practice in their camel talk and in the mix of English and Somali words. Farah and I had led the students into bilingual writing. It seemed a natural way to introduce the Somali language and help orient the Centerpoint students toward their upcoming encounters with their High Falls pen pals. A few students asked a bit enviously, "Did the High Falls students own camels?" Farah, who taught there as an aide, shook his head and for a moment looked sad.

The next morning, Farah reported that he and his Somali ESL (English as a Second Language) evening class had talked about camels for an hour. Camel-talk, for me, conjured up oases and palm trees, but for them it evoked pastoral lives that were probably lost forever. Somalia had greatly changed because of the war. As a boy Farah had heard lions—*li-baax*—roaming the northern part of the country outside his boarding school. "You know," he said, "a hungry lion, a *libaax*"—he gave the Somali word with its throaty *aa* and *x/h*—"a hungry *libaax* knows no fear. It will enter a village in the dark and snatch a small animal, sometimes a child." He paused. The students were watching him intently. "One night a *libaax* came close to our sleeping hut at school," he resumed. "I was awake and heard the roar and the heavy breathing. We were sleeping with open windows. I was worried about our donkey, and also about my own safety." The students' eyes widened. "But men were gathering outside. The lion ran away to the next village, and it was captured." I imagined a tawny, low-slung beast prowling a village street, sniffing at dooryards and the corners of houses.

It was an image out of *The Arabian Nights*—an image totally at variance with Farah's heavy Minnesota sweater and rubber-soled shoes. "Now, because of the civil war"—Farah shook his head—"all the big animals have left. Like the people, they have gone to safety in Kenya, where they are protected." He sighed. "The war has ruined our paradise," he said softly.

Later, this sentiment emerged from some of the Centerpoint students' poems. Jessica S. wrote, "I am part of our uncertain world in all different directions." The Centerpoint students had not yet met their pen pals at High Falls, but they were gathering sympathy for the wrenching changes many of the African students had lived through.

Notes on Writing Bilingual Animal Poems

Step 1. With Farah teaching, it was natural to engage in a dialogue, asking about camels and having him answer. Such a dialogue could be conducted by a teacher without firsthand experience of the animal by using maps, picture books (or videos, etc.), and foreign-language vocabulary. So, for example, an English-speaking, American teacher could introduce other African animals as we did the camel, with words in an African language for teeth, feet, ears, fur, roar, etc. Stories about an animal's habits and interactions with humans add interest to anatomical details. Domesticated animals will provide more human-centered stories than will wild animals. But oral histories, perhaps even photographs and commentary from American travelers to Africa or other continents, can help bring unfamiliar wild animals alive.

This exercise can also focus on birds or animals from the forests, plains, or oceans of North America. It might be compelling, for instance, to teach students the Native American names for a deer's hooves, hide, tongue, bones, etc. Invite into class someone who works with injured wild animals or who protects their habitat, to act as another kind of resource. Select animals outside a class' normal experience; for instance, whales for Midwestern students or buffalo for coastal students. Key to introducing all such animals, birds, or reptiles are stories about their behavior. Temperament, struggles for food or water, dangers from other animals or humans, favorite hideouts or forms of play—all sorts of true-to-life tales bond us with animals and help us write about them in a caring, imaginative, personal way.

Step 2. The exercise begins with dialogue. Then the students draw the animal, the teachers list unfamiliar words on the board, the experts tell stories about the animal, and finally the teachers or students read aloud a poem about the animal. The poem can provide suggestions for style and tone. For example, Farah and I selected several traits of the Somali camel poem to emphasize: addressing a friend, listing camel behavior and anatomy, and concluding with praise or summary. We also had the students use their camel drawings to help make comparisons. "What else does it look like?" we encouraged kids to ask about bits of their drawings. Gavin's "hump like a sunset" came from this activity. At their heart, the camel poems enthusiastically introduced an unknown animal from a number of perspectives, with the casual, friendly tone of one neighbor talking to another.

II.

As it flows past the warehouse district of Minneapolis, the Mississippi River spills over St. Anthony Falls. Near the falls, the High Falls school was housed. Bundled up to my eyes, I stepped into the warmth of its brilliant blue lobby. A camel batik hung in the office, where several boys conversed with elderly Somali men in embroidered hats.

High Falls was formed to help retain ties to Somali and Oromo culture. After several years of planning, it opened with aides speaking both languages, and its administration and staff composed of people with American and/or African educational backgrounds. When students suffered the inevitable dislocation of adjusting to the foreign ways of the United States, the staff could help in the students' native tongues. As had happened at Como High, High Falls also benefited from advice on post-traumatic stress syndrome when representatives of the Minnesota-based Center for the Victims of Torture visited. Especially in the school's earlier years, students had come from the Kenyan refugee camps, where simple survival required constant attention.

To help inform me about Somali culture in U.S. schools, I turned to *Accommodating and Educating Somali Students in Minnesota Schools: A*

Handbook for Teachers and Administrators, by Mohamed Farid and Don McMahan,[4] which showed, in clearly written classroom vignettes, the strengths and difficulties of the Somali immigrant community. Many children and adults had only recently left the chaotic uncertainties of the Kenyan refugee camps, and family members had often been lost in civil war. For many, a strong religious faith helped carry them through these hardships.

With every year, High Falls had fared better. The strong commitment of parents had made the school a center for many kinds of community activities. Likewise, the staff's dual representation of African and American cultures signaled a strong emphasis on communication, respect, and rich learning. Though many students had experienced some schooling before immigration, those whose lives had been most disrupted by civil war "have never held a pencil," one teacher told me. Like the Hmong language, written down in the 1950s, Somali had become a written language only in the 1970s, though before the war many Somali and Oromo had learned Arabic to read the Qur'an. High Falls' knowledgeable bilingual staff and firm discipline had helped students and parents deal with confusion and outbursts of anger. Sometimes single mothers whose husbands had been killed in the civil war worked to establish extended families of their own and other relatives' children. They received help and support from the school. Likewise, the school honored Muslim religious traditions around prayer, food selection, women's dress, Islamic holidays; the staff also guided students and parents in selecting what was important to learn about American culture, discouraging more superficial elements that students might try to mimic without parental supervision.

Now Farah and I, fresh from our three January days at Centerpoint, turned toward planning for our collaboration at High Falls. "Somali students are bound to be very talkative," Farah advised me. "The younger ones, born in the U.S. or in the refugee camps in Kenya, are fairly fluent in English. But the older ones who had to escape during the war—they struggle with the language." His own English was so excellent, rich in vocabulary, contemporary slang, and complicated syntax, that I found it hard to believe that other Somalis would not be equally skilled. But Farah had spoken English in Somalia and Kenya, years before he came to America. Sometimes he had to search for a Somali word, but rarely for an English one.

As we talked, it seemed natural to ask about his family. "Are you married? Do you have children?" Smiles wreathed his face and he leaned forward, nodding yes to both. Then the smiles faded, and worry lines crossed his forehead. His wife had worked until their first child, a son, was born. Farah shook his head and wiped his hand across his brow. "Immediately we learned why Americans have only two children. My, my, my," he exclaimed, "it is so expensive to have children in the United States." Now, since he had to work several jobs, his lonely wife had decided to spend the remaining months of her second pregnancy with her mother in London. A look of faraway sadness crept into his eyes. Farah would visit for the child's birth, but that was five months away. His own parents had been separated by the Somali civil war. His father had returned to Somalia, but his mother lived with a daughter in Kenya. Somalia was still chaotic; only the northern part with more years of self-government had settled into a semblance of order.

When we had first started planning the Centerpoint–High Falls poetry collaboration, I'd proposed that we write poems in two voices, which could be assembled into dialogue poems when the two groups of students finally met. The camel poems had been part of this preparation, and we had also written prefatory two-voiced poems with an accelerated class of Centerpoint students. Their two-voice poems about wildly divergent topics—walruses and pencils, to name just two—would help us introduce the process when the two groups of students met. Now we were in the humorous predicament of having to come up with an animal for the High Falls students to write about.

Dogs simply would not do. The Somalis distrusted dogs and considered them unclean. "If a dog sniffs my trousers," Farah explained, "I must wash them. Our people stay clear of dogs." What about horses? I had read several vivid poems about horses in the anthology of Somali poetry. In my initial approaches to Somali and Oromo culture, it had appeared that horses might be as important to their nomadic life as camels. Farah shook his head. Horses were familiar to Somalis in times past, but he doubted the students from the refugee camps would know much about horses today. Yet we had introduced camels to Centerpoint students, and they had been thrilled to learn about a new animal. It would probably be fine to introduce the High Falls classes to an animal they didn't know. The very lack of familiarity might fuel the students' interest.

Our horse poems began in a fifth grade taught by Mr. Paul. (High Falls students called their teachers "Mr. Paul" and "Miss Anna.") Mr. Paul's classroom was small, but the students were relatively small also, the boys wearing American-style clothes, and the girls wearing flowered or monochrome hijabs and skirts over winter pants. Farah had been right: the students were *very* talkative. Most fifth-graders like to talk; the High Falls students talked with their whole bodies. Hands shot out, heads bent for whispered intimacies, faces grimaced, feet stamped, eyes sparkled or clouded over. Voices tumbled in cascades of excitement or anger, especially the boys'. But within a few minutes Mr. Paul had the students in their seats, and Mr. Farah was introducing our model horse poem by Raage Ugaas. Son of a chief and educated in an "itinerant college," Ugaas was one of the most beloved of Somalia's traditional poets. As early as 1899 his acclaim had been described by Italian explorer Luigi Robecchi-Bricchetti, who recorded his death as a "brave warrior." Ugaas wrote about horses with the pride and authority of a monarch of the sands. Like the earlier camel poem, this one, "A Horse Beyond Compare," ran to three pages in the original; it also began as if spoken directly to an audience. No doubt the poem had been memorized and recited by friends of the author, as befitting the oral way of publishing poetry in pastoral Somalia.

Farah was a wonderfully expressive reader. But before he began, he told the class that now it was their turn to write about an unusual animal, and he showed pictures of both camels and horses, which he'd downloaded from the Internet. Eager to do exactly what their pen pals at Centerpoint had done, the High Falls class chanted, "Camel, camel" over and over. With gentle firmness, Farah and Mr. Paul subdued them, and Farah promised that if they were quiet and respectful, he would show them a movie. "*Sea Biscuit*," he said; "we will show you *Sea Biscuit*." Who knew if they had ever heard of the screen version of the Depression-era racehorse's story? But the promise of a movie gave them a pleasurable goal. Quiet was restored, and Farah could begin to read. Attuned at once to the poem and to the changing dynamic of the classroom, he quickly shifted from reciting to motioning toward a talkative student. At crucial moments, he repeated phrases for emphasis.

> When there's a "horse" poem to be made,
> There are some men who are held back
> As if confronted by a "cliff."
> . . . .
> So I shall compose some praises for my horse Walhad
> And start them with the sound of "waw."
>
> [Note: "Horse" was "equestrian" in the text. We changed it
> to an easier word. "Cliff" was "precipice" in the original.]

Farah stopped. "What is the horse's name?" he asked, and the class chanted "Walhad." "And what sounds do many words in the poem start with?" Farah called. "Waw," shouted the students.

> Is Walhad not as swift as if he were hurled from a sling?
> . . . .
> Does he not move with the speed of a message
> Whose words are sent by wire?

Farah stopped. "You remember the call across the ocean when you talk to Grandma or Auntie?" he asked. "Your voice goes this fast," Farah's hand whooshed through the air. "*That* is the speed of Walhad."

> His temper is hot, for that is his nature ...
> For if the man who holds the drinking pail
> Should motion him away before he has had his fill
> In a fury he will set upon that man ...
> Is he not like a bull rhinoceros?
> . . . .
> His color has the beauty of the sky
> When it is spread out to dry after rain
> . . . .
> He brings me nourishment and good fortune
> For when I ride him, whatever I am pursuing
> Becomes like ...
> Roads fiercely pierced by spears of rain ...
> —Raage Ugaas[5]

Farah called out, "Who has felt spears of rain?" All the boys' hands went up. Farah asked, "What is the color of 'sky hung out after rain'?," and a number of girls murmured, "Gray or blue?" Another complained, "But that's not a color of a horse." It was one of the liveliest discussions of a poem I'd ever encountered, partly because the call-and-response kept us all interested. The discussion also suggested the differences in boys' and girls' traditional upbringing. The boys could claim that they had felt "spears of rain" because in rural Somalia, boys spent far more time outside in the bush, herding animals, than did girls. As soon as they were old enough to help, the boys joined their male kinsmen in long treks from home. On the other hand, a traditional Somali girl stayed by her mother's side until she married. It was not surprising that the girls would think more about color, beauty, and design than the boys. It was also interesting that the girls in Mr. Paul's class challenged the comparison of the horse to the color of sky after rain. Did they know more about horses than we had expected?

The drawing step in the process (which the Centerpoint students had loved, especially the girls) brought Mr. Paul's fifth-grade class to queries and uncertainty. Many students asked teachers for drawing help. When Farah drew a horse on the board, I had to laugh. With a self-deprecating grin, he erased it and confessed that, like most of the students, he had never drawn in school. The Muslim prohibition against reproducing human or animal forms in art[6] had, I assumed, fostered the Somali oral tradition instead. We quickly switched to writing, the students calling out ideas and phrases as they went.

Their drafts shone with exaggeration and brilliant comparisons. After hearing Farah read the Walhad horse poem a second time, I recognized its exaggerated metaphors. After that, with other classes, mostly fourth-graders, Farah and I encouraged metaphor making. On their own, the students coupled exaggeration with metaphor. This seemed a particularly sophisticated strategy and I remembered that they were the heirs of poetic duelists, who tried to top each other with eye-popping similes. From "eats like a monkey" to "fast as the wind" to "fast as invisible" to "temper hot as boiling water," to the celestial speed of "He kicks the sun in the sky like/a cheetah running"—it was heartening to hear Somalia's tradition of literary exaggeration sounding on the frozen banks of the Mississippi. The students needed no one to tell them of a cheetah's speed or to teach them cocky po-

etic one-upmanship or pride in animals. Several of the older boys gave their
horses fierce resistant strength as if to ward off attackers.

> My horse is speedy
> fast as a cheetah
> eats like a monkey
> the color of blood
> smells like wind
> he's *meela*, he's speedy
> —Mahad, 5th grade

> My horse is so fast it can run on water
> it is so fast it is invisible
> its name is bullet
> it's too fast for you!
> —Mohamud, 5th grade

> My horse Black Beauty is as black as chocolate
> Black Beauty is as beautiful as a rose
> She has a diamond shape above her eyes
> Her hair is as soft as silk
> She runs as fast as a rabbit
> And as peaceful as the sun
> —Sartu, 4th grade

> My horse is named Donkey. He is
> fast as the wind. He is bright
> as the colors of rainbows.
> His temper is as hot as boiling water
> He kicks the sun in the sky like
> a cheetah running.
> —Shuaib, 4th grade

All the fifth-grade boys wanted to read aloud, and the fourth-grade girls
volunteered as often as did the boys. Puzzling over this, I remembered that
in traditional Somali life Western-style women's rights had made few in-
roads;[7] they might even have seemed superfluous. Furthermore, poetry in
Somalia had been more a preserve of champion male poets than of women
in general; in fact, the two genders wrote separately, only by chance hearing
each other's work. But this was the United States. Adorable Sartu, tiny as a
little *dik-dik* (an East African antelope), called her horse "Black Beauty"

probably because she had read the American story. Yet, her simile "peaceful as the sun" filled me with contentment and hope, a sunny, African kind.

With the fifth grade, we tried immigration poems, similar to those we had already written at Centerpoint. Though the immigrations represented in the two schools were separated by decades or more, we hoped that writing about journeys to America would foster common expressions and understanding. In these poems, we asked students to link colors with the feelings prompted by weather, modes of transportation, and change of location. When Mr. Farah told his own immigration story, the talkative fifth-graders gave him rapt attention. Then they peppered him with questions.

One student, Abdurahman, conveyed the essence of Farah's story, lending it his own spectrum:

> From Nairobi by plane to New York
> to Minnesota, gold happy to be
> in the U.S.A. Black sad to leave
> relatives behind. Silver embarrassed
> because I fell down. Every winter
> I feel cold beige.

Many students had stopped other places in the U.S. before reaching Minnesota. Their journeys to Maryland, Ohio, Missouri, Texas, California, made them "feel normal white" (Mohamed); "glad rainbow ... mad/to leave relatives behind" (Mahad); "happy like a yellow flower to be here" (Kafia);

> mad black when somebody
> comes up to me. I beat them
> up and they cry and I feel nothing.
> —Jalatama

Farah had been a good model for the class, describing his early pratfall, slipping in his slick African shoes on an icy Canadian sidewalk, and shivering in his thin trousers. Like him, the students hated snow.

> ... blue happy to be in Africa
> then ... in Minnesota I was
> green shy. White snow makes me
> angry like red.
> —Abdullahi

Notes on Writing Lyric Immigration Poems

Step 1. It's important to begin with telling an immigration story. Farah was our storyteller and all the students found his account fascinating. Next I asked him to put colors to some of his experiences. This introduced the idea of infusing a lyric element into the often harsh and wrenching experience of immigration. We then asked students to practice associating colors with moods and experiences. "What color fits loneliness?" or "What color captures the experience of seeing a new land for the first time?"

Step 2. After practicing some of these associations, we divided immigration into several segments: reasons for leaving, saying goodbye, things left behind, experience along the way, arrival in new places, the mistakes or embarrassments, shocks or comforts of the new. We tried to help students make these rather abstract categories more concrete, such as mentioning the weather on the leave-taking, or memories of home, or first sights of the new world. The students at Centerpoint had discussed their families' immigration histories at home and brought this information to school. The students at High Falls were writing about themselves, for the most part, or about Farah; thus their association of colors with various segments of the immigration experience was more immediate. To help the Centerpoint classes make personal connections with their families' more remote stories of immigration, I suggested that they imagine themselves as one of their ancestors, and write in the first person. Thus they put themselves on the ship or inside the airplane that brought their relatives to North America.

Step 3. At High Falls, each student wrote a short poem, selecting some of the segments of immigration to associate with colors. At Centerpoint, we had time to write classroom ballads, generating choruses from Farah's story of leaving Somalia, staying in the Kenyan refugee camps, and arriving in Canada, and then using the students' short poems about their own families' experiences as the verses. Had we had more time with the High Falls students, we would have woven their short individual poems into a ballad, as well. Ballads have the advantage of joining an entire class' work into one poem, which can then be read aloud, chorus alternating with verse, in a public celebration of shared experiences.

III.

At last the day arrived for the students at High Falls and Centerpoint to encounter each other. Our last day at High Falls, the fourth-grade girls had
asked nervous and excited questions about their pen pals from Centerpoint. They had enjoyed the months of e-mail and snail-mail correspon-
dence. The encounters began at Centerpoint for purely logistical reasons.
The students from High Falls arrived late, and stood awkwardly in their
puffy winter coats while Centerpoint teacher Sandy Harthan introduced
them to their partners, with whom they'd been corresponding. From the
sidelines, Farah and I watched these now-familiar kids. Some were shy and
nervous, twisting paper or looking at the floor. Others, loud and boisterous, cuffed each other on the arm or immediately launched into long conversations. After lunch—the High Falls students eating from their lunch
bags and the Centerpoint students being served a bag lunch—the students
broke into three groups. One went outside for sledding; it was a bright, cold
Minnesota day. A smaller group did an art activity with Centerpoint
teacher Karla Harding, and another smaller group wrote poems in two
voices with us.

Sitting on the conversation bleachers—a slender High Falls boy paired
with a burly Centerpoint boy, a tall High Falls girl beside a petite Centerpoint girl—the kids quickly reviewed what they knew about camels and
horses. The exuberant High Falls boys were rather subdued beside their
Centerpoint counterparts; a few sat apart from each other, but the majority
of boys crowded onto the carpeted bleachers, busily asking to borrow
pencils, shouting out names of video games, even "vroom-vrooming" the
engines of their family SUVs. It was the girls who looked more different
from each other. Pretty in their flowered or monochrome hijabs, the Somali High Falls girls wore undercaps and long, flowing scarves. It was impossible to see any of a girl's hair or ears. In contrast, most of the
Centerpoint girls wore typical unisex American outfits of jeans and sweat-
shirts. Only their hairstyles claimed uniqueness: bobs, long ponytails, curls.
Perhaps it was this contrast as much as anything that made the Somali girls
seem very lady-like. They sat demurely on the floor while their Centerpoint
counterparts jumped up, tossed their ponytails, or called questions across
the room.

To get the ball rolling, we read them my favorite poem-in-two voices, "Grasshoppers," from Paul Fleischman's book *Joyful Noise: Poems for Two Voices*[8]:

Sap's rising	
	Ground's warming
Grasshoppers are	Grasshoppers are
hatching out	hatching out
Autumn-laid eggs	
	splitting
Young stepping	
	into spring.
Grasshoppers	Grasshoppers
hopping	hopping
high	
Grassjumpers	Grassjumpers
jumping	jumping
	far
Vaulting from	
leaf to leaf	
stem to stem	leaf to leaf
plant to plant	stem to stem
	Grass-
leapers	leapers
Grass-	
bounders	bounders
	Grass-
springers	springers
Grass-	
soarers	soarers
Leapfrogging	Leapfrogging
longjumping	longjumping
grasshoppers	grasshoppers.

Then, because this delightful poem was hard to teach quickly to a somewhat distracted bunch, we handed out blue copies of a "Walruses" poem-in-two-voices, written by two Centerpoint students. It was simpler in its two-voice rhythm, and its language was less complex, with no compound words or different phrases repeated simultaneously. Reading aloud

in two voices was an immediate hit: short High Falls boy/tall gangly Centerpoint boy; large, pink-flowered High Falls girl/wiry, jeaned Centerpoint
girl; the shy with the loud, the meek with the confident, the equally paired
(which made me smile at the marvel of chance). We could have continued
reading Nicole and Isabella's "Walruses" poem all day. Simply reading
aloud was a fun, bonding experience for the students. The Centerpoint kids
helped if a High Falls student stumbled over a word; a High Falls student
radiated enthusiasm if a Centerpoint student shrank back. The "Walruses"
model had simplified and clarified some of the strategies, including labeling the two voices at the top, with an option for both voices indicated in the
middle. Words for different voices occurred on alternating lines, and when
both voices spoke, their shared words were placed down the middle of the
page.

Walruses

VOICE 1	BOTH	VOICE 2
	Walruses are	
fat		
		cute
yellow tan		
		crew cut
	Walruses are	
mammals		
		swim
slow		
		swimming
	Walruses eat	
	poor fish	
	Walruses	

—Nicole and Isabella

It was time to try our camel-horse poem experiment. At the desks, with
big sheets of paper, the students labeled the various voices. Each High Falls
student was in charge of writing a horse section for a poem in two voices,
and each Centerpoint student in charge of a camel section. Of course, there
were hundreds of ways to approach the pairing of information and the process of writing. We encouraged the students to take turns, giving each one
in the pair a chance to write.

VOICE 1	BOTH	VOICE 2
Camel		Horse
	blubber face	
breadlike feet		hooves
	They kick	
	They spit	
hissing		neighing
live without water		
for a month		
	water	
		fast
trot		
	feet	
		run
carries family		
		no humps
	wild	
	Brain the size of a	
	Bird	
	—Ishrafeel and Nic	

I liked the common traits being spoken by both voices. Though I don't remember each student with great clarity, Ishrafeel stood out for his excellent command of English. His unusual name, calling up Romantic poetry, had made me wonder where his parents had found it. Likewise, I had to wonder where these boys had gotten the idea that four-footed animals had brains the size of birds. Hearing it, I laughed. And smiled as the two read their final draft, earnest and proud of their accomplishment, almost the same height.

VOICE 1	BOTH	VOICE 2
Camels		
	and	
		Horses
like		
	water.	
		Horses
have		
	hooves.	
		Camels
have		

bread-

like

     feet.

           Horses

run

     fast.

           Camels

     trot.

Camels

     have

           humps.

Horses

     do

           not.

    —Sarah and Roda

Sarah and Roda had taken an entirely different approach to using the two voices: they broke sentence statements into single words spread across the three options of performing them. I did not recall either girl, which made me sad when I selected their poem to include in this book. I told myself it would have been impossible to make descriptive notes of all the students as they read, but in retrospect, I wished that I had tried.

Tanner and Mohamud used wonderful comparisons, not the only ones to do so, but by far the most vivid:

VOICE 1	BOTH	VOICE 2
Camel		Horse
walks slow as a		
tortoise		
		runs like lightning
	trot	
brown as sand		
		black as night
	water	
desert dry		
as the sun		
		farm as wide as you
		can see
	You can ride them.	

The two-voice-poem activity was almost a complete success as a community-building activity. Students enjoyed working together; few argued. They especially enjoyed performing their poems for me or Farah. Sitting first with the mixed groups of students at the Centerpoint school, and then at High Falls, we listened and marveled at the different mixtures—a shy Centerpoint boy paired with a bold High Falls one whose English might not be so good, but whose pizzazz was outstanding, or a small, brightly clad High Falls girl paired with a paler and taller Centerpoint girl. In most cases, the students seemed to have forgotten their differences or used them to help the project along.

Notes on Two-Voice Poems

This is such an oral exercise that it's easy to forget that writing is at its center. Only with very advanced writing students would I create a poem-in-two-voices without writing preliminary list poems first. Thus, the Centerpoint and High Falls students used their earlier camel and horse poems as stepping-off points for the joint venture. Even so, it was important to do some brainstorming at the start of class, having one group introduce the camel and the other the horse while a teacher put words on the board. Equally crucial was the experience of reading aloud the several examples of poems-in-two-voices. In fact, we gave each student copies of the "Grasshopper" poem and the "Walruses" poem. This helped them visualize how to set up their collaborative poem and showed them some strategies for playing words among the two voices. We used big sheets of blank paper and recommended that the students fold the sheets into three segments. They labeled the segments Voice One, Both, or Voice Two. Farah and I helped many pairs get started by suggesting bits from their individual poems that they could use. We emphasized that repetition created a songlike quality; we urged spreading words or sentences across two voices; and we repeated the direction to take turns, a "camel" writer starting a line and a "horse" person finishing, or vice versa. Many students wanted to try their first few lines aloud. After we had listened, they added more lines. It was a very noisy but productive time.

For our last two days of paired teaching, Farah and I stumbled onto a wonderful way to teach a nursery rhyme from Somalia that used the Somali names for the fingers. Farah taught the finger names first. It was astonishing that many of the Somali students did not know the words in Somali for the fingers. Growing up in times of crisis, frequently on the run, the Somali students rarely had the leisure to learn nursery rhymes. Wanting to be inclusive, we brought in one of the Oromo aides, who gave us the finger names in Oromo. At the beginning of this activity, I led some finger play, first making shadow puppets—the alligator of Peter Pan with his ticktock; then the interlaced hands of "Here's the church, here's the steeple, open the door and there're all the people" of my childhood (with a modification to "Here's a mosque, here's a dome..."). We tried clasping hands and turning them inside out, then wiggling our pointer fingers in an exercise that's called "Brain Gym." Next Farah introduced the Somali names for the fingers:

- Thumb: *Suul Gambar, suul* is thumb, *gambar* is a stool; all the other fingers stand up, the thumb sits on a stool.
- Pointer or index finger: *Murugsato*; licking finger. Somalis eat with their hands, thus this is the finger for licking.
- Middle finger: *Fardhexo*; *far* is finger, *dhexo* is tall.
- Ring finger: *Fadumo*; also a girl's name
- Pinky finger: *Faryaro*; *far* is finger, *yaro* is little
- Palm: *Baabaco*: "where no hair grows."

It was amusing to watch the American kids try to get their rather stiff, English-speaking lips around the double *a*s of the juicy word: *Baabaco*. Sitting on the big teacher's desk, holding up his fingers as he spoke, Farah grinned and almost smacked his lips with the pleasure of saying the finger names.

- "*Waylaha aroori yoo.*" Take the calves to the water. And Farah held up all five fingers and began marching into the other hand.
- "*Ceelka qaraar ku du woo.*" Do not take them to the sour well. The sour well was the elbow joint. By now the fingers had marched up the arm and paused at the elbow.
- "*Ceelka macaan u di.*" Take them to the sweet water, which was way under the arm, where tickling and laughter commenced.[9]

I mentioned that in English we had a toe-playing rhyme that involves pigs. Since we didn't take off our shoes, the Centerpoint students demonstrated with their fingers.

> This little piggy went to market,
> This little piggy stayed home.
> This little piggy had roast beef,
> This little piggy had none.
> And this little piggy went
> Wee wee wee all the way home.
> (Then the baby is tickled on the bottom of its feet.)

We talked about how Somalis and all Muslims don't eat pork, don't like pigs, and won't have them around their yards. Naturally, they would not have a rhyme about taking piggies to market. But they do herd calves, and water is a huge part of life in the dry country. Sour water is desirable for camels, but calves need sweet water.

After the pairs of High Falls and Centerpoint students drew their hands facing each other, or all facing into the center if there were more than two in the group, they decorated their hands. We talked about the language of hands: scars, lifelines, and fingerprints. "Manual" means hands (*le mani* in Italian). We asked the students to write the Somali finger names, and two additional lines linking their fingers or palms with some other element, like a decoration (many of the Somali fourth-grade girls had henna designs lightly stamped on the backs of their hands), or an activity which the finger or hand accomplished.

For each class of paired students, I typed up a class collection of finger lines, without indicating who wrote them. Here are some:

> I can twist my hands like an armadillo
> *Faryaro, Fadumo*
> Finger push-ups, sleeping snakes
> *Fadumo, Fardhexo*
> I can make hills with my hands
> I decorate my hands with henna.
> *Fardhexo, Murugsato*
> Pointer finger, licking finger
> I hold the horse reins with my hand.

Murugsato, Suul Gambar
Thumb like a stool

Suddenly, as we were engaged in talking about pigs and piggies, Farah remembered the wild boars of Somalia, warthogs with curved tusks. "The last time I was home," he recalled, "our car was stampeded by these wild pigs. We thought if we hit them, one would roll up on the car and damage us." As if prompted by this distant memory, Farah began reading one of his own poems to the class. It was one I'd seen him working on recently; in fact, a week ago, as we had waited for the High Falls students to arrive at Centerpoint, he had sat quietly at a computer. I had thought he was answering e-mail. But no, he rose and showed me a heavy piece of paper where he had composed an impassioned plea for his country. It began with an evocation of the waterboys calling the camels to the watering hole, much as we had discussed a month before with the Centerpoint students. It then expanded into a cry of frustration, like a thirsty camel, gone a month without water, bellowing at the water trough gone dry. The politicians make promises that they do not keep; the land is still torn with war and disunion.

As he read to the joined class of High Falls and Centerpoint students, the class, mainly boys, listened intently. When he stopped, one boy, who had known the Somali names for the fingers before Farah said them, called from the back of the small room, "It makes me sad." Another boy echoed this feeling. "It is our country," he added. A very small boy said, "There was a war. I wasn't born, but my parents had to walk through the war. I [they] lost my father's picture." Another voice continued, "We were walking away from the country, and my big sister was supposed to be behind us. I heard an explosion and looked around. She was lying dead on the floor." Shocked, Farah said, "She stepped on a mine." The boy did not appear to know what this meant but confirmed, "Yes. She lay dead on the floor."

It was impossible to gauge the students' response to this sad repetition because the buses had come and we had to break apart. I thought of all the unknown times the students' lives had been jolted apart, leaving fragments to return at odd moments such as the one we had just experienced. Leaving abruptly, I felt keenly the unfinished nature of all teaching. And I wished especially for these students a continuous, less fractured flow to their lives.

Notes on Hand Drawing and Writing Activity

Big pieces of paper are essential, allowing two or three students to arrange their hands in an interesting pattern and then draw around them. The hands can face each other across the paper, or rise together like ferns from the bottom, or angle in from the corners. Next, have students write the foreign words for the fingers and other parts of the hand. Then discuss what distinguishes hands: fingerprints, scars, jewelry, shape of fingernails, decorations or words written on the hands, plus the lines inside the palm. Ask students to draw some distinguishing elements on their hands. Then have them consider what their hands are good at, or bad at; difficulties the hands have created for the person; sounds hands can make; what hands dream of; and any other fanciful experience hands might have. Ask students to write two or three lines about the life of their hands. These lines can curve around the drawings of the hands, or zip like arrows off the fingertips, or march sedately at the bottom of the page. For a finale, print or type up a group poem with lines from each collaborative page, interspersed with the foreign words for parts of hands.

NOTES

[1] The Oromo are the largest cultural and language group in Ethiopia, with centuries of conflict among various Oromo groups and Ethiopian rulers, invading Islam jihadists, European colonialists, and peoples from surrounding countries. Under Ethiopian emperor Haile Selassie, the Oromo were oppressed and driven off their lands. Famine from the 1970s to the 1990s, as well as systematic imprisonment and torture sent large numbers of Oromo refugees into Somalia, Kenya, and from there into Europe and the Americas. The Oromo and the Somali share cultural traits, including about 30 percent of their words in common. See Gadaa Melbaa, *Oromia: An Introduction to the History of the Oromo People* (Kirk House Publishers, 1988, 1999).

[2] My knowledge of traditional and newer Somali poetry was substantially enhanced by *An Anthology of Somali Poetry*, translated by B. W. Andrzejewski with Sheila Andrzejewski (Indiana University Press, 1993).

I also read portions of John William Johnson, *Heelloy: Modern Poetry and Songs of the Somali* (Haan Publications, 1996).

Background on the relation between recent political developments in Somalia and its poets came from Alexander Stille, "The War of the Words," *Granta 75 Brief Encounters*, 2001.

[3]Cumar Xuseen "Ostreeliya," "Where True Profit Lies," *An Anthology of Somali Poetry*, pp. 72–75.

[4]Mohamed Farid and Don McMahan, *Accommodating and Educating Somali Students in Minnesota Schools* (Hamline University Press, 2004).

[5]Raage Ugaas, "A Horse Beyond Compare," *An Anthology of Somali Poetry*, pp. 9–12.

[6]Farid and McMahan, *Accommodating and Educating Somali Students*, pp. 38–39.

[7]Ibid., p. 8.

[8]Paul Fleischman, "Grasshoppers," *Joyful Noise: Poems for Two Voices* (HarperCollins Children's Books, 1992, pp. 3–4).

[9]I have several versions of this rhyme, which was written hastily on chalkboards by Farah and copied hastily by me. The spelling varied, but not the oral and dramatic effect as Farah taught it to the students and they chanted it and made the accompanying actions. I suspect, but did not ask, that Farah may never have seen it written down. Since Somali was created in a standard orthography during the 1970s, when Farah was a child, he may have learned it entirely from oral memory. The rhyme thus may suggest many of the hallmarks of Somalia's oral poetic tradition, with its enjoyable emphasis on group participation and "publication" through memorization and repetition.

CONCLUSION

I rarely learn the end of a school story. For the brief time we're together, a week or two weeks, the stories of teachers and students become my stories. Initial impressions etch toward revelation; shy students speak out, and the boisterous bow their heads over desks. As pencils scratch on paper, I stand back and breathe a sigh of relief. Once more the alchemy of inspiration and encouragement has sped a current of belief and excitement through words. Even on difficult days, when disruption or fragmentation disheartens me, I often discover, reading the students' poems in cramped motel solitude, how brightly the poems shine.

A teacher friend recently reported hearing ELL guru Stephen Krashen distinguish language learning from language acquisition.[1] Language learning involves "skill-building" and mistake correction; it is a painstaking process of memorization and repetition. But language acquisition is another thing entirely: when language play occurs, students begin to strut. On the classroom stage, or on sidewalks, in malls, on the ice, they gesture inside new garments of words and syntax. Cloaks droop or sway, mope or jig. Alcides, a Hmong student from Argentina, whirls inside a rain forest cafeteria, with monkeys, leopards, and himself feeling American at the end of the year. Another student knits herself inside two different hues and cadences: one side sings in New World Spanish, the other rounds English to mimic its lively tongued neighbor.

Bringing language down off the chalkboard, creative writing connects words with environment and history; it allows prairie students to infuse renditions of hunting or cultural change with the sough of prairie wind. It sparks jazzy rhythms of city buses and gritty quarters. We poets have always known this. We know how to play the best of a language (English or Spanish or Somali) against political/commercial/textbook reductions.

Tell the truth but tell it slant—

Success in circuit lies ...
        —Emily Dickinson

Yet, there are failures. An entire class stymies us. A community whose voice has been suppressed does not speak, even to us. A community with a lingo we don't know will fall silent in our presence. Eric L., who grew up near my friend Beth Slocum's farm in Vasa, Minnesota (home of an early American Swedish Lutheran church), complained bitterly about his high-school English classes, twenty miles away in the medium-sized city of Red Wing, population 16,000. Though he was extremely good at math and physics, Eric was reduced to being a shy farm boy in English class. He couldn't make heads or tails out of Shakespeare or *Silas Marner* or suburban and urban poets. He wanted to read about haying. He wanted to write a research paper on raising sheep. If I had been teaching Eric's class, he'd probably have felt left out.[2]

Gradually in my twenty-five-plus years of residency teaching, I've learned, in education parlance, to meet students "where they are." Through inspiration and necessity, I've discovered that there is sometimes a special switch to light classes that would otherwise have remained in the dark. Yet Eric's story nags and makes me sad. Though we creative-writing guests sometimes evoke secrets, and may surprise talent out of its den, we aren't magicians enough on our own to overcome hierarchies of prejudice and the dicta of textbooks geared to national averages. We need classroom teachers savvy and forthright enough to set us straight. We relish the almost unbearable lightness of teaming with dual-language poets and educators who know their immigrant students inside out. Since these children and young adults now sit in schools around the country, my hints about how to meet them where they are, and my reports of the delicious writing that results—bilingual, tri-cultural, quadri-national—all bear spreading around.

During my years of circuit writing, many school districts have built in-house writing power plants. This book is for them as well as the lone teachers who burn the bulb of creative writing in their own buildings. All of us who teach—circuit writers, classroom mavens, district experts—can benefit from discoveries that splice the circuits of language and repair some broken fuses. Over the twenty-five years that I've been on the road to writing discovery, I've been enriched, as teacher and writer, by new classrooms I've encountered. As I reach through the dark to meet students "where they are," I've also discovered the colorful diversity of life in Minnesota, which offers so much more than Nordic-tinged accents and hot-dish potluck suppers.

In Minnesota our winters are long, warmer now, we're told, but still dark, dark. We can't all play hockey on dazzling white ice. We need the glow of the arts to substitute for Nature's green.[3] Upstairs in my winter study, sun spills over the tissue-paper feathers of a papier maché parrot, a present from an Ada, Minnesota, third grade. When I entered their classroom, I found twenty green-and-blue parrots dangling over the kids' heads. It was a no-brainer. All I had to do was let poetry complete the circuit that was already dangling, waiting to be caught. My bird's knowing black eye, its forward beak, point toward a nearly life-sized bust some kid drew of me, head topped with beret slightly askew, and turquoise earrings swaying. On my chest a message beckons: Poetry Reading, March 14th, 4th and 5th Grades.

These are the endings that light my way home: an auditorium filled with parents and younger sibs in sand-crusted boots. Winter coats hang over hijabs or overalls; the welcome may sound in Somali, Spanish, and English; the "lunch" consists of juice and coffee, "bars" or "fry bread."[4]

Newly fledged poets step up to the microphone. There is a hush. Some race through their lines; others take it slow. Light spills over their heads. Humor and metaphor are sweet. The next word pierces the dark. This time, finding your way will be a breeze. I know I'm on the right route.

NOTES

[1]Stephen Krashen has published extensively on language acquisition and use. See, for example, *Explorations in Language Acquisition and Use: The Taipei Lectures* (Crane Publishing Company, 2002); "The Input Hypothesis and Its Rivals," in *Implicit and Explicit Learning of Languages* (Academic Press, 1994, pp. 45–77); *Principles and Practice in Second Language Acquisition* (Prentice Hall, 1982).

[2]Interview in Vasa, Minnesota, with Eric L., December 2002.

[3]Arts in education has become a national pastime. Since I first went on the poetry circuit, arts of puppet theater and classical Javanese court dance, mural and "landfill" arts, Native American drumming, cartooning, photography, and videography—all have taken to the road. Daniel Gabriel, program director for arts in education at COMPAS and a fiction

writer himself, notes the array of language-based arts residencies: storytelling, spoken word, songwriting, "performance poetry," even writing about ancient civilizations with kids making papyrus and clay tablets for cuneiform and hieroglyphics. For the past twenty years, COMPAS has consistently funded an average of 170 weeks of artists-in-the-schools residencies each year. COMPAS currently lists sixty artists on its roster; the Minnesota State Arts Board roster includes seventy. Though public funding for arts residencies has decreased about 20 percent, according to Amy Frimpong, arts in education director for the Minnesota State Arts Board, many more organizations have a stake in arts residencies in schools. (Phone interviews with Daniel Gabriel and Amy Frimpong, April 2006.)

[4]"Fry bread" is a term for fried dough, which becomes puffed and crispy and which is served and enjoyed by many Native American groups and their guests.